MW01155839

DATE DUE

GAYLORD			PRINTED IN U.S.A.

Bloom's Modern Critical Interpretations

Bloom's Modern Critical Interpretations

Bloom's Modern Critical Interpretations

Carson McCullers'
THE BALLAD OF THE SAD CAFÉ

Edited and with an introduction by
Harold Bloom
Sterling Professor of the Humanities
Yale University

CHELSEA HOUSE
PUBLISHERS
A Haights Cross Communications Company
Philadelphia

©2005 by Chelsea House Publishers, a subsidiary of
Haights Cross Communications.

A Haights Cross Communications ◢ Company

Introduction © 2005 by Harold Bloom.

All rights reserved. No part of this publication may be reproduced or transmitted in any
form or by any means without the written permission of the publisher.

http://www.chelseahouse.com

Printed and bound in the United States of America

10 9 8 7 6 5 4 3 2 1

Library of Congress Cataloging-in-Publication Data

The Ballad of the Sad Café / Harold Bloom, ed.
    p. cm. — (Modern critical interpretations)
  Includes bibliographical references and index.
  ISBN 0-7910-8125-7 (alk. paper)
  1. McCullers, Carson, 1917-1967. Ballad of the sad café. I. Bloom, Harold. II. Series.
  PS3525.A1772B35 2004
  813'.52—dc22
                                                                        2004012648

Contributing editor: Janyce Marson

Cover design by Terry Mallon

Cover: © Pam Ingalls/CORBIS

Layout by EJB Publishing Services

All links and web addresses were checked and verified to be correct at the time of
publication. Because of the dynamic nature of the web, some addresses and links may
have changed since publication and may no longer be valid.

Every effort has been made to trace the owners of copyrighted material and secure
copyright permission. Articles appearing in this volume generally appear much as they did
in their original publication with little to no editorial changes. Those interested in
locating the original source will find bibliographic information in the bibliography and
acknowledgments sections of this volume.

HARPER COLLEGE LIBRARY
PALATINE, ILLINOIS 60067

Contents

Editor's Note

My introduction centers upon *The Heart Is a* Lonely *Hunter* as well as *The Ballad of the Sad Café*, finding in each, Carson McCullers' curious strength in representing a universal hunger for love, however grotesquely that hunger manifests itself.

John McNally relates the *Ballad*'s narrator to Joseph Conrad's Marlow, who sets the archetype for finding a story's meaning in its outward aura. For Joseph R. Millichap, the ballad indeed is a clue to the novella's literary genre, and also to its vision of what might be judged a demonic love. A comparison to D.H.Lawrence informs Panthea Reid Broughton's reading, in which rejection of the feminine enhances the isolation of every individual.

A comprehensive scholar of McCullers, Margaret B. McDowell finds mingled humor and pathos in the *Ballad*, while Louise Westling properly treats the narrative as its author's masterpiece, and Mary Ann Dazey analyzes the narrator's two antithetical voices.

McCullers' vision of eros is compared to those of Katherine Anne Porter and Eudora Welty by Ruth M. Vande Kieft, after which Margaret Whitt ponders the song of the chain gang in the *Ballad*.

Clare Whatling interprets Gothic elements in the *Ballad*, while Doreen Fowler finds Freud's Primal Scene of begetting in the novella.

This volume's final essay, by Sarah Gleeson-White, examines elements of androgyny in both *The Heart is a Lonely Hunter* and the *Ballad*.

HAROLD BLOOM

Introduction

"I become the characters I write about and I bless the Latin poet Terence who said 'Nothing human is alien to me.'" That was the aesthetic credo of Carson McCullers, and was her program for a limited yet astonishingly intense art of fiction. Rereading her after nearly twenty years away from her novels and stories, I discover that time has enhanced *The Heart Is a Lonely Hunter* and *The Ballad of the Sad Café,* and perhaps rendered less problematic *Reflections in a Golden Eye.* What time cannot do is alter the burden for critics that McCullers represents. Her fiction, like her person, risked that perpetual crisis of Eros of which D.H. Lawrence was the poet and Freud the theoretician. Call it the tendency to make false connections, as set forth by Freud with mordant accuracy in the second paragraph of his crucial paper of 1912, "The Dynamics of Transference":

> Let us bear clearly in mind that every human being has acquired, by the combined operation of inherent disposition and of external influences in childhood, a special individuality in the exercise of his capacity to love—that is, in the conditions which he sets up for loving, in the impulses he gratifies by it, and in the aims he sets out to achieve in it. This forms a *cliché* or stereotype in him, so to speak (or even several), which perpetually repeats

1

and reproduces itself as life goes on, in so far as external circumstances and the nature of the accessible love-objects permit, and is indeed itself to some extent modifiable by later impressions. Now our experience has shown that of these feelings which determine the capacity to love only a part has undergone full psychical development; this part is directed towards reality, and can be made use of by the conscious personality, of which it forms part. The other part of these libidinal impulses has been held up in development, withheld from the conscious personality and from reality, and may either expend itself only in phantasy, or may remain completely buried in the unconscious so that the conscious personality is unaware of its existence. Expectant libidinal impulses will inevitably be roused, in anyone whose need for love is not being satisfactorily gratified in reality, by each new person coming upon the scene, and it is more than probable that both parts of the libido, the conscious and the unconscious, will participate in this attitude.

All of McCullers' characters share a particular quirk in the exercise of their capacity to love—they exist, and eventually expire, by falling in love with a hopeless hope. Their authentic literary ancestor is Wordsworth's poignant Margaret, in *The Ruined Cottage*, and like his Margaret they are destroyed, not by despair, but by the extravagance of erotic hope. It is no accident that McCullers' first and best book should bear, as title, her most impressive, indeed unforgettable metaphor: *The Heart Is a Lonely Hunter*.

McCullers' few ventures into literary criticism, whether of Gogol, Faulkner, or herself, were not very illuminating, except in their obsession with loneliness. Her notes on writing, "The Flowering Dream," record her violent, physical response to reading Anne Frank's diary, which caused a rash to break out on her hands and feet. The fear of insulation clearly was the enabling power of McCullers' imagination. When she cited Faulkner and Eugene O'Neill as her major influences, she surprisingly added the Flaubert of *Madame Bovary*, where we might have expected the Lawrence of *The Rainbow* and "The Prussian Officer." But it was Emma's *situation* rather than Flaubert's stance or style that engrossed her.

The most remarkable of McCullers' conclusions is the vignette called "The Twelve Mortal Men" that serves as epilogue or coda to *The Ballad of the Sad Café*:

THE TWELVE MORTAL MEN

The Forks Falls highway is three miles from the town, and it is here the chain gang has been working. The road is of macadam, and the county decided to patch up the rough places and widen it at a certain dangerous place. The gang is made up of twelve men, all wearing black and white striped prison suits, and chained at the ankles. There is a guard, with a gun, his eyes drawn to red slits by the glare. The gang works all the day long, arriving huddled in the prison cart soon after daybreak, and being driven off again in the gray August twilight. All day there is the sound of the picks striking into the clay earth, hard sunlight, the smell of sweat. And every day there is music. One dark voice will start a phrase, half-sung, and like a question. And after a moment another voice will join in, soon the whole gang will be singing. The voices are dark in the golden glare, the music intricately blended, both somber and joyful. The music will swell until at last it seems that the sound does not come from the twelve men on the gang, but from the earth itself, or the wide sky. It is music that causes the heart to broaden and the listener to grow cold with ecstasy and fright. Then slowly the music will sink down until at last there remains one lonely voice, then a great hoarse breath, the sun, the sound of the picks in the silence.

And what kind of gang is this that can make such music? Just twelve mortal men, seven of them black and five of them white boys from this county. Just twelve mortal men who are together.

The rhetorical stance or tone of this is wholly McCullers', and is rather difficult to characterize. In context, its reverberation is extraordinary, working as it does against our incapacity to judge or even comprehend the grotesque tragedy of the doomed love between Miss Amelia Evans and Cousin Lymon, with its consequence in the curious flowering and subsequent demise of the sad café. We, as readers, also would rather love than be loved, a preference that, in the aesthetic register, becomes the defense of reading more intensely lest we ourselves be read, whether by ourselves or by others. The emotion released by the juxtaposition between the music and its origin in the chain gang is precisely akin to the affect arising from McCullers' vision of the tragic dignity of the death of love arising so incongruously from the story of Miss Amelia, Cousin Lymon, and the hideous Marvin Macy.

JOHN McNALLY

The Introspective Narrator in
"The Ballad of the Sad Café"

Carson McCullers' novella, *The Ballad of the Sad Café*, is intriguing for a number of reasons. First there is the incredibly grotesque gallery of characters who people the little dreary town in which the story takes place. Then, of course, there is the enigmatic epilogue, "The Twelve Mortal Men," which seems at first glance to have been an afterthought of the author. And there is the disturbing plot with its love triangle so reminiscent of Sartre's curious *menage à trois* in *No Exit*. But perhaps the most disturbing feature of the whole novella is the point of view which informs the piece.

On the surface of it, the narration of *The Ballad of the Sad Café* is third-person omniscient with an occasional authorial intrusion. The narration employs the present tense for three introductory paragraphs, shifts to the past tense for the whole flashback section—virtually the whole story unfolds in this section—and returns to the present tense for the final three paragraphs, two of which comprise the chain-gang epilogue. Simple? Yes. And no.

Yes, the point of view is simple at first glance; however, a careful examination of the tense-shifts, the so-called intrusions and digressions, and the appended "Twelve Mortal Men" shows that McCullers has fashioned a very complicated fictive narrator from whom the reader receives the details of the story and about whom he is left to speculate. When one reads the

From *South Atlantic Bulletin* 38, no. 4 (November 1973). © 1973 by the South Atlantic Modern Language Association.

novella in the understanding that the narrator is a character in the story, he notices a subtle but significant shift in the story's form and subsequent themes. Such a reader finds himself absorbed not so much with the bizarre goings-on in the old café as with the changing perceptions of a person in the process of intense introspection—a process he shares with his listener-reader.

The first clue to the actual point of view is the fact that the story begins and ends in the present tense. In itself, the present tense does not a fictive narrator make. Considered in the context of the references to "here" and "now," though, the use of the present suggests a person who is describing the café "on the spot." For example, in the first paragraph the narrator says "the winters *here* are short and raw," and "*here in this very town* there was once a café," suggesting his presence on the scene he is describing (italics mine throughout). Then, speaking of the café which "has long since been closed," he says that "it is still remembered." In not pointing out who specifically in the town remembers the café, he suggests that it is he, the narrator, who remembers it as he sits there looking at its boarded up remains. A further suggestion of the narrator's actual physical presence comes from the comment that on "*These* August afternoons— ... there is absolutely nothing to do; you might as well walk down to the Fork Falls Road and listen to the chain-gang." In referring to "*these* August afternoons" the narrator places himself in a more or less specific time; in suggesting that you "*walk down* to the Fork Falls Road and listen," he fixes himself in space. He is in the town, most probably right in front of the café on an August afternoon which is "white with glare and humming hot."

To perceive the narrator as an actual person who is in the little town on a hot August afternoon is not merely to observe one of the story's nicer nuances. To read the story in the light of this perception is to read a very different story indeed—it is to read a story in which, for one thing, the apparent authorial intrusions and digressions are no longer flaws in the narrative but actually key passages in the story's curious network of meanings.

When the narrator "digresses" to explain the significance of the whisky, for example, he now takes on the credibility of one who has actually tasted of it and felt its effects. Now he is one who knows from experience that the whisky is "clean and sharp on the tongue" and that "once down a man it glows inside him for a long time afterward." He is one who *knows* that the experience of drinking Miss Amelia's liquor is one in which a person is "shown the truth;" he, himself, is a person who has "warmed his soul and seen the message hidden there." As an actual character, then, the narrator is less to be faulted for digressing than would a simple omniscient narrator— for *real* people do digress when they tell stories.

But there is more to this than mere verisimilitude. As the concern of a character-narrator, the "digression" is more clearly related to the later section in the story in which the narrator describes the effects of the music of the chain gang. For, just as Miss Amelia's liquor had once "warmed his soul," "shown the truth" and the "message hidden there," so now the music causes his "heart to broaden," his soul to "grow cold with ecstasy and fright." The café he had once visited gone, the narrator seeks truth in the music of the earth itself," of the "twelve mortal men who are together."

Besides the liquor "digression" and the enigmatic chain-gang passage, there are other frequent points in the narrative at which the narrator asserts his personality—points at which he speaks directly to the reader (or, perhaps, a fictive listener) to tell him, in effect, to pay attention, to remember this detail or that, to see things this way or that. Fairly early in the flashback section of the story, the narrator says "Now this was the beginning of the café.... It was as simple as that. *Recall* that the night was gloomy as in wintertime." Somewhat later he says, "for the moment regard these years from random and disjointed views. *See* the hunchback marching in Miss Amelia's footsteps.... *See* them working on her properties.... So *compose* from such flashes an image of these years as a whole and for a moment *let* it rest." Still later, the narrator says "So *do not forget* this Marvin Macy as he is to act a terrible part in the story which is yet to come." In each of these instances the tone is clearly conversational, the mild imperatives suggesting direct address. We may not *see* the narrator as a character at this point, but it is virtually impossible not to *hear* him as one.

If in these passages the narrator reveals something of himself, what is it? In other words, who is he? What does he mean?

It should be remembered that in the second paragraph of the story, the narrator suggests that "you might as well walk down to the Fork Falls Road and listen to the chain-gang." At this point the comment smacks of cynicism: given the choices of staying or leaving, one might as well leave, for, after all, there is nothing to do. But the narrator doesn't leave—not yet. Intrigued by the setting or, perhaps, merely discouraged by the August heat, he stays to reminisce (To himself? To a listener? Who can be sure?) about the café that once was. It is here that the verbs shift tense and the café and its people come back to life—but they are seen through the filter of the narrator's power of recollection. The whole story he remembers—digressions and all—has the effect of changing his perceptions of himself and his present predicament. He realizes, for example, that the characters he has recalled were incapable of sharing love, that each was the other's hell. He recalls a pageant of grotesquery and violence that eventually turns the nostalgia to bitterness and pain. More than anything else, though, he experiences the contrast between the proprietress in her prime and the bent, broken and inward-turned terrible face she now shows at the window.

The recollection done, he is a man who sees himself in the town in which he sits, who sees the town—like the remembered café—as a reflection of his own static image. It is here—after the flashback—that he repeats "Yes, the town is dreary...." It is so dreary that "the soul rots with boredom." It is so dreary that he "might as well go down to the Fork Falls highway and listen to the chain-gang." This last paragraph suggests, then, that the narrator is a man who realizes he has refused to obey his impulse to move—to go listen to the chain-gang. It shows him to be a man who has wrestled with the past and who has used the past to reinterpret the present. It shows that he knows that when nothing moves—the spirit dies; "the soul rots with boredom."

The so-called epilogue, "The Twelve Mortal Men," seen in the context of the character-narrator's struggle becomes not a cryptic appendix to a gothic tale but, instead, the positive act of a man of changed perspective. In this section the narrator fulfills his own earlier inchoate suggestion to "go down to Fork Falls highway and listen to the chain-gang." This time, though, there is less of the cynicism which characterized the initial suggestion—for now to go to listen is to save one's soul from rotting. The whole section is seen in direct contrast to the flashback section of the story. Where in the café reminiscences the narrator found free people unwilling or incapable to share love with one another, in the epilogue he finds people in chains who share their suffering and who, in sharing, bring music from the earth and sky. Such music is what keeps the narrator's soul alive.

It has not been my purpose here to insist that the inside story—the flashback about the café that is still remembered—is of minor significance. On the contrary, that story is an intriguing one: it is a grotesque delineation of love's power to destroy. It *has* been my purpose, though, to show that its chief significance lies in what it reveals about the character who, in recalling it, gives it its shape and who, in reaction to it, finds new meaning in his own existence.

Let me call on the narrator in just two more instances to help make my position clear. At one point in the story, the narrator says something which could easily be taken as a key to this story's significance. "There are great changes," he says, "but these changes are brought about bit by bit, in single steps which in themselves do not appear to be important." Then, later, speaking of Marvin Macy, he provides what, I believe, is a clue to his own situation. "But though the outward facts of this love [read: story] are indeed sad and ridiculous, it must be remembered that the real story was that which took place in the soul of the lover [read: narrator] himself."

What we have in *The Ballad of the Sad Café*, then, is a beautifully sculptured piece of writing in which we overhear the internal monologue of a character whose haunting recollections enable him to overcome his own *ennui* and to resist the atrophying pressures of the familiar world; a character to whom, like Marlow in Conrad's *Heart of Darkness*, the "meaning of an episode was not inside like a kernel but outside, enveloping the tale which brought it out only as a glow brings out a hare, in the likeness of one of those misty halos that sometimes are made visible by the spectral illumination of moonshine." The *Ballad* is a song of the human spirit.

JOSEPH R. MILLICHAP

Carson McCullers' Literary Ballad

Carson McCullers' novels, particularly *The Heart Is a Lonely Hunter* (1940) and *Member of the Wedding* (1946), often have been misread as Gothic and grotesque fictions, categories derived by critics from her works in these modes, *Reflections in a Golden Eye* (1941) and *Ballad of the Sad Café* (1943). Strangely enough, the same critics, intent on demonstrating their Procrustean theories in all of her work, often misunderstand *Ballad* by insisting on the universality of elements which are obviously peculiar to the point of aberration. The use of the bizarre theory of love offered by the narrator of *Ballad* as a formula for interpreting all of McCullers' fiction has hampered analysis not only of the *novella* itself but of her other works as well. The description of her narrative as a ballad, so obviously presented in the title, provides a key to understanding which unlocks the novella's difficulties of literary mode, point-of-view, characterization, and plot structure.

The literary ballad evolved from the ballad of tradition, which in turn is rooted in folklore, because the literary artist wished to exploit the archetypal energy of the ballad world and the formal simplicity of the ballad structure. Professor Gerould, the best known authority on the ballad, has provided in *The Ballad of Tradition* a succinct definition based on a wide knowledge of the *genre*. "The ballad is a folk song that tells a story with stress on the crucial situation, tells it by letting the action unfold itself in event and

From *The Georgia Review* 27, no. 3 (Fall 1973). © 1973 by the University of Georgia.

speech, and tells it objectively with little comment or intrusion of personal bias." Though McCullers' ballad is neither song nor folk art, and though its narrator certainly intrudes a great deal of personal opinion, the narrative also presents many of the characteristics Professor Gerould mentions in his definition and develops in his elaboration of it. McCullers' ballad concentrates on the strange love triangle formed by a manly giantess, a selfish dwarf, and a demonic bandit. The action unfolds in a few weird events which culminate in an epic battle waged purposely on Groundhog Day to decide the death or rebirth of love. The setting is a romantic wasteland where piney woods and swamps counterpoint the stunning heat of August afternoons. The concrete symbols of the ballad world both explain and motivate the action; buildings lean in precarious decay; trees twist grotesquely in the moonlight; birds and animals provide mysterious analogues to human action.

Clearly this is the traditional world of the ballad, a world of passion and violence, of omens and portents, of the full wild impulsiveness of archetypal human behavior. The particular world of this ballad is a Georgia mill village, a place like all the Southern back country, "a place that is far off and estranged from all other places in the world." The Southern hinterlands preserved the folk qualities as well as the folk songs of the Scotch border country. Therefore, the line between the real world and the ballad world is often indistinct in the American South and in McCullers' fictions which are set there. Unlike the larger mill city which serves as the setting of most of her fiction, the mill village is not used to probe economic conditions or regional problems in a realistic manner. Even the chronological setting is unimportant; it might be 1920 or 1940; for the village in *Ballad* exists in the temporally imprecise world of human passion.

Of course, McCullers' ballad is a literary one, wrought by a modern, conscious artistry not by the folk mind or by an artless imagination. The literary ballad has always been a difficult form; it can be hauntingly effective, as in Keats' "La Belle Dame Sans Merci," resoundingly dull, as with many of Scott's attempts, or unintentionally humorous, as Longfellow's "The Wreck of the Hesperus." The structural and stylistic integrity of the story, especially of narrative voice marks her literary ballad as an unqualified success. McCullers presents a narrator who can spin the fine fabric of romantic fiction from the raw materials of mill-village life without violating either realm. In *Ballad* a ballad-maker evokes from the world of the Georgia back-country a timeless, compelling story of human passion. His voice fixes the style of the novel—a perfect blend of the literate and colloquial, the objective and personal, talky observation. The existence of this filtering personality assures the novella's achievement.

Neither McCullers nor the typical third person omniscient voice, narrates; the ballad-maker tells the tale. A part of the town himself, he knows people, places, and history, often commenting like a chorus of spectators from the village (the refrain of the ballad sometimes has this same function). At the same time he is possessed of knowledge that only an omniscient author could have. Therefore, he must be creating the narrative from the history of this particular mill-village and demonstrating the operations of human passion to his listeners.

This device also releases McCullers from responsibility for the universalization of the fantastic observations on the mutual exclusiveness of love so often ascribed to her by earlier critics (such as Oliver Evans, Ihab Hassan, and Klaus Lubbers). The narrator defines love as "joint experience between two persons," the lover and the beloved. The experience between them is not necessarily the same for each party, for the lover and the beloved "come from two different countries." The lover attaches his love to some person, often without rational purpose. He creates an imaginary world surrounding the beloved and then releases his stored creative energies on this dream vision. "Therefore, the value and quality of any love is determined solely by the lover himself." The narrator continues: "It is for this reason that most of us would rather love than be loved. Almost everyone wants to be the lover. And the curt truth is that, in a deep secret way, the state of being beloved is intolerable to many. The beloved fears and hates the lover, and with the best of reasons. For the lover is forever trying to strip bare his beloved. The lover craves any possible relation with the beloved, even if this experience can cause him only pain."

The ballad-maker's theory of love is substantiated by the character relationships in the novella, but the limited number of cases prevents immediate acceptance of it as a universal law of human nature; it clearly remains the narrator's hypothesis, not McCullers'. The theory depicts one facet of the love's dynamics, but other loves have other patterns. In her later novels and stories love does live for a few people, at least for a time. Yet the earlier novels have partially demonstrated this pattern. In *Heart*, Singer often lashes out against the lonely hearts, who have forced themselves on him as lovers, though he is most often simply puzzled by their behavior. The tangled relationships of *Reflections* are sometimes marked by hate, for example, Leonora's hatred of Capt. Penderton, but most often by indifference. In the limited context of this novella, the ballad world, this one tragic aspect of love is exaggerated to the point where it looms as its totality. The ballad creates a picture without delicate shading; therefore, the projection of one tragic aspect of love can be accepted romantically as the whole definition of this complex human phenomena. The same fascinating effect exists in many of the traditional ballads, in "Barbara Allen" for instance, where an analogous love–hate relationship exists between the courtly lover and the disdainful beloved.

The narrator's theory of love arises out of the weird triangle that forms the structural center of this novella. There are three characters of importance: Miss Amelia Evans, Cousin Lymon, and Marvin Macy. Miss Amelia is loved by Marvin Macy whom she rejects; she loves Cousin Lymon; he turns from her to an idolatrous love for Marvin Macy, who despises the dwarf. A neat triangular diagram is formed.

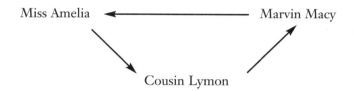

The ballad relates the story of this diagram, and the story aptly illustrates the ballad-maker's generalizations about love. As in both *Heart* and *Reflections* a geometrically patterned relationship of characters is the basis of symbolism and structure.

After the description of the town, which opens the tale, the narrator introduces Miss Amelia. On the hot, empty afternoons of August, the season when the town seems most desolate and isolated, her strange face peers down crazily from an upper window of the town's largest structure which is now boarded up and fast decaying. The building has "a curious, cracked look that is very puzzling," and Miss Amelia's haunted face with her severely crossed eyes provides the human analogue of the structure. The ballad-maker is also the Southern storyteller, the courthouse or country store loafer who will pass this dull August day retelling the story of the building and its strange inmate. The third paragraph introduces the history of the café, and of Miss Amelia, Cousin Lymon, and Marvin Macy. The narrator wanders back to the misty times before the café even existed; the ballad is being spun.

Earlier the café had been a store which Miss Amelia had inherited from her widowed father; "Big Papa" had raised the motherless girl almost like a son. The big-muscled Amazon easily assumed her masculine role and even surpassed her daddy in becoming the leading entrepreneur of the region. She supplies the mill workers and the surrounding farmers with groceries, hardware, and sundries. She also produces for sale her own chitterlings, sausage, sorghum, and whiskey. The quality of her versions of these Southern staples, especially her whiskey, is superior to any others; in fact the liquor becomes almost a magic potion which creates joy and insight. "For the liquor of Miss Amelia has a special quality of its own. It is clean and sharp on the tongue, but once down a man it glows inside him for a long time afterward. And that is not all. It is known that if a message is written with lemon juice on a clean sheet of paper there will be no sign of it. But if the paper is held for a moment to the fire then the letters turn brown and the meaning becomes clear. Imagine that the whiskey is the fire and the message is that which is known only in the soul of a man—then the worth of Miss Amelia's liquor can be understood." Miss Amelia is also the doctor, sawmill operator, and major property owner of the mill-village. Supernatural elements are present in her doctoring, as Miss Amelia's cures are drawn from the folk medicine of the region and her own mysterious researches into the properties of roots and herbs. Her benevolent or white witchcraft adds to the magical atmosphere of the tale. (An example is her use of "pot liquor," the juices left in the pot after cooking vegetables, as a rub for Lymon's frail body; Southern folk superstition still attaches magical healing powers to this brew.) Her whiskey and her medicine are also representative of a basically human, creative nature. Yet there is another side of her always competing with these generous instincts. She is acquisitive and avaricious in all her business dealings, quick to "go to law" or to use her big fists to defend her property rights. The store stands as her citadel; its transition into a café is essentially the story of Miss Amelia's humanization through love.

She has an earlier chance for human contact in her marriage, but it proved a dismal failure. Marvin Macy, her husband, is another larger-than-life character, as legendary in the mill town and its environs as Miss Amelia. An unhappy childhood caused by irresponsible parents made him into a figure of evil. His corruption is belied by his physical appearance. "For Marvin Macy was the handsomest man in this region—being six feet one inch tall, hardmuscled, and with slow gray eyes and curly hair." Moreover he is materially successful with a good job as a loom-fixer at the mill. Yet beneath these bright surfaces some dark force impels him to acts of outrageous evil. He carries as a talisman the salted ear of a man he killed in a razor duel, while another pocket contains "marijuana weed." As the demon lover of the region, he has degraded the sweetest young virgins, performing these depredations as coolly as he cuts the tails off squirrels in the pine woods. Yet Miss Amelia, because she is essentially unfeminine, cannot be seduced; Marvin confuses her asexuality and father fixation with personal strength, and this mistake makes him love her. He imagines that her self-sufficient strength can turn him from his dissolute ways, make him a responsible person, and restore the happiness he lost in childhood. In fact, he is asking her to be a mother to him, to replace his own lost mother.

The incestuous undertones of his love are mirrored in Miss Amelia's acceptance of him; she simply wants someone to take Big Papa's place as a companion and business partner. Both Amelia and Marvin project their unconscious desires onto the other, and both will be mightily disappointed. Marvin's love for Amelia does have an immediately reformative effect, and, until she rejects him, he is serious and well-behaved. Miss Amelia, hating him for his love, despising her own feminine role, and always driving a hard bargain, never allows their marriage to be consummated, not even when Marvin wills her all his possessions, and after ten days she drives him off her property.

Cousin Lymon is the strangest member of this outlandish trio. His past is mysteriously clouded; there can be no proof of his own version of his history, and even the village loafers regard it suspiciously. He does not elaborate in any way on his first revelation. When asked where he has come from, he replies uncertainly, "I was traveling." Even his appearance conceals the past of this mysterious stranger.

> His eyes were blue and steady as a child's but there were lavender creepy shadows beneath these blue eyes that hinted of age. It was impossible to guess his age by his hunched queer body. And even his teeth gave no clue—they were all still in his head (two were broken from cracking pecans), but he had stained them with so much sweet snuff that it was impossible to decide whether they were old teeth or young teeth. When questioned directly about his age the hunchback professed to know absolutely nothing—he had no idea how long he had been on the earth, whether for ten years or a hundred! So his age remained a puzzle.

The dwarf has much of the child about him. He possesses "... an instinct to establish immediate and vital contact between himself and all things in the world." His child's love of treats and spectacles—movies, fairs, cock-fights, revivals—provides insight into his personality, as does his child's curiosity and quarrelsomeness. Thus in many ways Cousin Lymon seems akin to the fairy children of folk tale and ballad—pixies, elves, leprechauns.

Miss Amelia is attracted to him by these childish qualities. Among people she likes only "the nilly-willy and the very sick," those she can see as easily molded and changed by her strong hands. In a sense the sickly, childish dwarf appears pliable. His physical deformities are also part of his attraction for Amelia and the others; touching a hunchback's hump is regarded as good luck in folk tradition. He becomes a strange combination of man, child, and pet that Amelia can love as she could not love her husband. He is a man loved without sex, a child acquired without pain, and a companion which her limited personality finds more acceptable than a husband or a child. Their relationship, like Amelia's marriage, is symbolically incestuous and immaturely formed.

The very nature of her attitude toward him ultimately causes his rejection of her for Marvin Macy. Some bond of natural kinship exists between the two adolescent men. When they first see each other they exchange a stare, "... like the look of two criminals who recognize each other." Cousin Lymon has a child's fascination with outlaws and an adolescent's admiration of the rebel and outcast. More importantly, the criminal is a father figure; Marvin Macy's tall, straight body and masculine swagger are qualities opposite to Lymon's, qualities which are not a part of the child's role he must play with Amelia. Therefore, he begins to reject Amelia, just as Marvin Macy hates him as representative of his failed marriage. A new dimension of hate is added to the love triangle,

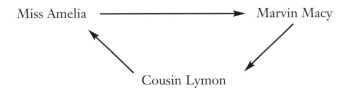

Plot is developed tightly and economically so as to dramatize the creation of these triangles and to emphasize the role of the balladeer-narrator. After beginning in the "present" with the description of the town, the narrator shifts back many years to the arrival of Cousin Lymon, the mysterious stranger who completes the triangle. The movement is natural; he switches to the beginning of the café in the relationship between Lymon and Amelia. This movement also initiates the temporal and seasonal motifs which form an important part of the novella's symbolism. Cousin Lymon arrives in April with the spring, symbolic of creation, youth, and love. When the villagers suspect that Amelia has murdered the tiny stranger the weather turns cold once again, but winter's gloom is dispelled by the warmth of the café when Lymon is discovered alive and well. Amelia's marriage took place in winter and the groundhog sees his shadow before the final battle, a portent of the triumph of hate over love and six more weeks of winter. The temporal shift at the opening is to the "once upon a time" past when things were happier, and the season is appropriate for Amelia's love creates the café and both flourish for the following six years.

The narrator quickly moves the story through these years of human growth for Miss Amelia, symbolized by the emergence of the café. Since the events of these years are ordinary and repetitive he merely summarizes them.

The seasons pass in their regular order, and the passage of time is productive of joy and love. The store evolves into a real café with tables and chairs, decorations, and a mechanical piano. Like Biff Brannon's New York Café in *Heart*, Miss Amelia's place has a spiritual function as well as a material one. At the café there were at least a few hours when "the deep bitter knowing that you are not worth much in this world could be laid low." Miss Amelia even neglects to lock the door; clearly a change has taken place.

The years pass in this fruitful manner until Marvin Macy comes back to the village; bad luck follows him to his home town. Though it is autumn the weather turns hot again at his return, spoiling the barbecue and chitterlings just made. A whole family dies from eating spoiled pork. The natural rhythms of the seasons are broken for the first time in six years, when Marvin Macy arrives with the fall like some Hades of Dixie bringing death, desolation, and waste. As the fall turns to winter Marvin Macy's fearful reputation increases, and in direct proportion so does Cousin Lymon's adoration of him. On January 2 it snows, a strange occurrence in the mill village, and Marvin Macy somehow assumes credit for this meteorological miracle. Miss Amelia in her agitation comes to hate Macy even more deeply than she has in the past. They often circle each other, fists clenched, in ritualistic fashion, and the community waits tensely for the conflict to explode. Miss Amelia's degeneration is symbolized by the poison she puts in Marvin's food; her witchcraft is now destructive, her magic black with hate. After the snow Cousin Lymon brings his beloved to stay in the rooms over the café; this final displacement of Amelia precipitates the total collapse on February 2, Groundhog Day. The date proves significant because Cousin Lymon sees the groundhog observe his shadow, an indication of six more weeks of winter ahead and a prefiguration of Marvin Macy's destructive triumph. Other portents are observed on this ominous day: "A hawk with a bloody breast flew over the town and circled twice around the property of Miss Amelia."

The climactic battle begins at seven o'clock, as Miss Amelia sets great store by the mystical number seven. Significantly the fight takes place in the café; the center of companionship and symbol of love has become a place of hatred and combat. The two fighters are evenly matched, and they lunge at each other like wildcats. After a half hour of stunning punches and wild kicks, they become locked in a fearsome wrestling hold.

The ballad-maker points out that this is the style of fighting natural to country people and that the heroic struggle will be decided by this contest of raw strength and will power. After several agonizing moments Miss Amelia emerges as stronger; slowly, she bends her opponent to the floor and gets a strangle hold on him. She has won. But at this instant of victory Cousin

Lymon springs onto her back, flying across the room like "a hawk," and turns the advantage to his beloved Marvin. Before the crowd can react Miss Amelia is severely beaten, and left in disgrace. She drags herself into the office, and the crowd disperses. Cousin Lymon and Marvin Macy leave that night, but, before they go, they completely wreck the café: food, whiskey, decorations, the mechanical piano. The café ends as Miss Amelia's love ends. Slowly she shrivels into an old maid; her muscles shrink and her eyes cross to look inward. After three years of lonesome waiting for Cousin Lymon to return, she has the store-café boarded up. Retreating into the upstairs rooms, she remains there alone and isolated. The town takes on a new loneliness also; a perpetual August drought envelops it in a claustrophobic malaise. Time hangs heavy and dull.

> Yes, the town is dreary. On August afternoons the road is empty, white with dust, and the sky above is bright as glass. Nothing moves—there are no children's voices, only the hum of the mill. The peach trees seem to grow more crooked every summer, and the leaves are dull gray and of a sickly delicacy. The house of Miss Amelia leans so much to the right that it is now only a question of time when it will collapse completely and people are careful not to walk around the yard. There is no good liquor to be bought in the town; the nearest still is eight miles away, and the liquor is such that those who drink it grow warts on their livers the size of goobers, and dream themselves into a dangerous inward world. There is absolutely nothing to do in the town. Walk around the millpond, stand kicking at a rotten stump, figure out what you can do with the old wagon wheel by the side of the road near the church. The soul rots with boredom. You might as well go down to the Forks Falls highway and listen to the chain gang.

The chain gang illustrates the prison house aspect of the human condition. The coda, entitled "Twelve Mortal Men," emphasizes how man can achieve creativity, in this case the beautiful work songs and ballads of the gang, even in the most difficult situations if there is harmony and cooperation. The last sentence of the novella points out that they are only "... twelve mortal men who are together." The picture of the chain gang contrasts with the reader's final vision of Miss Amelia. She could release her creative efforts when she was "together" with Cousin Lymon; alone she can accomplish nothing. Where love and harmony exist much can be created; sadly enough, they exist in few places and for short times—human failings quickly frustrate them, and they are often replaced by hate and isolation. McCullers' other novels demonstrate this condition in the modern social world; the strange ballad of the café that becomes sad traces the roots of these difficulties in the timeless province of the lonely human heart.

PANTHEA REID BROUGHTON

Rejection of the Feminine
in Carson McCullers'
The Ballad of the Sad Café

Well over a century has passed since Alexis de Tocqueville astutely observed that compulsive individualism, so idealized in America, might indeed foster personal isolation. Tocqueville surmised that the inescapable isolation of the individual American was as much economic as political and that, though its causes might indeed be material, its ultimate significance was spiritual; for Tocqueville concluded that, as it throws a man "back forever upon himself alone, [democracy] threatens in the end to confine [that man] entirely within the solitude of his own heart."[1]

The spiritual solitude Tocqueville sensed in the America of the 1830's has hardly lessened with the passage of years. Indeed, as our literature of alienation abundantly testifies, man's sense of isolation has been exacerbated in the intervening years. But the so-called literature of alienation frequently is so lacerated with hatred and self-pity that it fails to offer any really mature understanding of the phenomena of alienation. Not so with the fiction of Carson McCullers; for McCullers, who made personal alienation the explicit single concern of all her fiction, treats the solitude of the heart with both objectivity and compassion and, ultimately, with an understanding born of the blending of head and heart.

Mrs. McCullers once said of her work "my central theme is the theme of spiritual isolation. Certainly I have always felt alone."[2] In her *The Ballad*

From *Twentieth Century Literature* 20, no. 1 (January 1974). © 1974 by Hofstra University Press.

of the Sad Café,[3] the setting itself serves as metaphor for such spiritual isolation. She begins this novella by establishing the dreariness, lonesomeness, and sadness of a setting which seems "estranged from all other places in the world." The largest building in the town, we are told, is old, boarded up, and leans far to one side. The house has "about it a curious, cracked look" which results, we discover, from its having once been haphazardly half-painted. The house is not, however, uninhabited. On hot afternoons a face may linger at the window for an hour or so before the shutters are closed once more: "It is a face like the terrible dim faces known in dreams—sexless and white, with two gray crossed eyes which are turned inward so sharply that they seem to be exchanging with each other one long and secret gaze of grief." (p. 1)

All of this sounds curiously gothic. We have the impression that the town itself is a grotesque, warped by its isolation, and that the building, with its cracked appearance, its dilapidated one-sided construction, and its boarded-up façade, might serve as symbol for whatever life remains in it and in the town. For life here is hopelessly inward, separated, and estranged. Selfhood means only confinement in the solitude of one's own heart.

With D.H. Lawrence, Carson McCullers believed that "we need one another" and that we attain our very individuality itself in living contact, the give-and-take of human relations.[4] Lawrence felt that without such relationships, we are nonentities. In *The Ballad* McCullers presents us with an unnamed Southern town and with a woman, Miss Amelia Evans, who together almost manage to escape aloneness and nonentity. The effort, however, is as abortive as the abandoned paint job on the front porch of her house.

When the building Miss Amelia owns becomes a café rather than a dry goods store, Miss Amelia and the townspeople as well almost succeed in breaking out of their separateness. On the occasion when Miss Amelia first breaks her rule and allows liquor to be drunk on the premises, an atmosphere of "company and genial warmth" suddenly emerges. "For," McCullers writes, "the atmosphere of a proper café implies these qualities: fellowship, the satisfactions of the belly, and a certain gaiety and grace of behavior." (p. 16)

In other words, through the café people do manage to overcome their aloneness. They begin to share their liquor, and when the café closes, Miss Amelia for the first time forgets to bolt her door. Trust in one another, founded on a new sense of human dignity, pervades. The change may best be seen in Miss Amelia who, along with Cousin Lymon, becomes actually sociable and is "not so quick to cheat her fellow man and to exact cruel payments." (p. 17)

Most studies of *The Ballad* emphasize only McCullers' theme of spiritual alienation and irreparable loneliness; they seem to disregard the fact that aloneness was, for a time at least, actually overcome. But Carson McCullers is very explicit about the achievement of "an air of intimacy ... and a vague festivity" in the café. Her theorizing about the café is crucial enough to deserve quoting at some length:

> But it was not only the warmth, the decorations, and the brightness, that made the café what it was. There is a deeper reason why the café was so precious to this town. And this deeper reason has to do with a certain pride that had not hitherto been known in these parts. To understand this new pride the cheapness of human life must be kept in mind. There were always plenty of people clustered around a mill—but it was seldom that every family had enough meal, garments, and fat back to go the rounds. Life could become one long dim scramble just to get the things needed to keep alive. And the confusing point is this: All useful things have a price, and are bought only with money, as that is the way the world is run. You know without having to reason about it the price of a bale of cotton, or a quart of molasses. But no value has been put on human life; it is given to us free and taken without being paid for. What is its worth? If you look around, at times the value may seem to be a little or nothing at all. Often after you have sweated and tried and things are not better for you, there comes a feeling deep down in the soul that you are not worth much.
>
> But the new pride that the café brought to this town had an effect on almost everyone, even the children.... Children love to sleep in houses other than their own, and to eat at a neighbor's table; on such occasions they behave themselves decently and are proud. The people in the town were likewise proud when sitting at the tables in the café. They washed before coming to Miss Amelia's, and scraped their feet very politely on the threshold as they entered the café. There, for a few hours at least, the deep bitter knowing that you are not worth much in this world could be laid low. (pp. 40–41)

Although, then, the "people in this town were unused to gathering together for the sake of pleasure," they do manage for a time to do so and consequently to escape the humdrum everydayness of their lives and the sense of their own worthlessness. But the effort cannot be maintained; the café is closed and the people retreat once again into their own separateness and aloneness. The convivial nights in the café end ostensibly because Marvin Macy and Cousin Lymon have ransacked the place, carving obscene words on the tables and bringing shame and sadness to Miss Amelia. But I should like to suggest that the café's violent end was already inherent in the consciousness of Amelia and her patrons.

McCullers makes a comparison between useful commodities which have a clearly established value and human lives which do not. The comparison is seminal here[5] because it is a lack of confidence in their own human worth which renders the townspeople incapable of sustaining the transcendent affirmation which was the café. For the dreary desperation of the town with its one-industry economy has conditioned the people to hoard themselves as well as their money. As Tocqueville long ago surmised, spiritual isolation is closely aligned with competitive capitalism. Here the normative pattern for dealing with the world and its people is the transaction. Now the transaction may be efficient, abstract, uninvolved, and profitable, but it is also dehumanized. In the business transaction people are used, not respected. Their worth is calculated in terms of dollars and cents. Of course, as McCullers writes, there is "no feeling of joy in the transaction," only the determination not to risk too much. And so, among a people "unused to gathering together for the sake of pleasure" the experience of joy cannot be sustained. To expend the soul in an open give-and-take relationship with another is too much of a risk; it seems safer, and more expedient, to approach another only to take rather than to risk being taken.

The three central characters exemplify this habit of defining human relationships pragmatically. Ravishing the young girls in the town, Marvin Macy has exploited human relationships to assert his will. Miss Amelia has exploited them to make a profit. (We learn that until the arrival of Cousin Lymon, she has never invited anyone to eat with her, "unless she were planning to trick them in some way, or make money out of them.") And even Cousin Lymon, who has "an instinct to establish immediate and vital contact between himself and all things in the world," exploits these contacts for excitement; for Lymon, who loves a spectacle, tries to create tension in the café by badgering and setting hostilities on edge. Furthermore, each of these characters, when he is the beloved, only exploits the other's affection. Amelia appraises Marvin's gifts and then shrewdly puts them up for sale; Lymon uses his sickliness, like his trick of wiggling his ears, whenever he wants "to get something special out of Miss Amelia." And Marvin, of course, uses Lymon's devotion to get his own back from Amelia.

Now, John B. Vickery may suggest that there is comedy in the characters' inability to synchronize their successive roles as lover and beloved;[6] I would insist, on the other hand, that the situation is tragic. For these characters simply do not know how to love. As the lover, each is a slave; as the beloved, each is a tyrant. None can achieve a satisfactorily balanced human relationship. He cannot love without sacrificing his own individual integrity, nor can he be beloved without exerting his power and superiority. His problem directly results from the deeply ingrained assumption that one approaches a human relationship only to exploit, not to enjoy. These characters cannot overcome a value system in which it is better to subjugate than to share, better to use than to love. They live in the world that McCullers describes in her poem "Saraband:"

> The world that jibes your tenderness
> Jails your lusts.[7]

In this world, the virtues of openness, receptivity, tenderness, and compassion are held in such contempt that no one can comfortably express them.

In this town if a man shows his feelings he is labeled contemptuously, a "Morris Finestein;" Finestein, we are told, was a little Jew sensitive enough to cry whenever people called him a Christ-killer and foolish enough to live in this town (before, that is, an unnamed but easily imagined calamity overcame Finestein and he was compelled to move away to Society City). The reference to Finestein is important because it reveals the town's concept of sexual roles. McCullers writes "if a man were prissy in any way, or if a man ever wept, he was known as a Morris Finestein." (p. 5) In other words to be sensitive, to weep, is to be effeminate. The human virtues of tenderness and sensitivity are considered to be exclusively feminine and decidedly superfluous and downright contemptible by a pragmatic and rationalistic society. The human psyche has then been split, "cracked;" if you will, into qualities which are feminine and contemptible on the one hand and masculine and admirable on the other.

Sexual characteristics, then, are so rigidly dichotomized that they cannot be held in balance. One is either servile and feminine, or, preferably, dominant and masculine. Ideally, as the psychoanalyst Karl Stern writes in his study entitled *The Flight from Woman*, "Man in his fullness is bisexual,"[8] or, as Carson McCullers herself puts it, "By nature all people are both sexes."[9] But here, in this novella, people cannot be both sexes at once. Marvin Macy, for instance, who is described as the "cause" of all the trouble, is ruthlessly masculine. With his razor and knife and the sharpened stick he uses to pick his teeth, he is viciously phallic. McCullers describes him as an "evil character" with a "secret meanness" about him. She explains:

For years, when he was a boy, he had carried about with him
the dried and salted ear of a man he had killed in a razor fight. He
had chopped off the tails of squirrels in the pinewoods just to
please his fancy, and in his left hip pocket he carried forbidden
marijuana weed to tempt those who were discouraged and drawn
toward death. Yet in spite of his well-known reputation he was
the beloved of many females in this region—and there were at the
time several young girls who were clear-haired and soft-eyed,
with tender sweet little buttocks and charming ways. These
gentle young girls he degraded and shamed. (p. 20)

Macy, then, dominates and destroys others in order to enhance his own
ego. To admit his need of another is equivalent, in this frame of mind, to
abolishing his own ego. That is why Marvin Macy's attachment to Miss
Amelia is such a pathetic thing. Her indifference only provokes further, more
desperate, acts of self-abasement from him, but to no avail. Miss Amelia
continues to ignore the man Macy and to turn his gifts to profit. It is only
normative though, as McCullers remarks in one of her short stories, that
"you hate people you have to need so badly."[10] Thus Macy cannot but resent
Amelia, not only for spurning him, but for making him so despicably servile.
And so Marvin Macy vows to get even, and he does.

Macy's behavior represents the extremes of sadism and masochism
which Erich Fromm tells us are not emotionally dissimilar.[11] And I should
like further to suggest that his unhealthy behavior, whether aggressively
masculine or servilely feminine, results from a social ethos which has
destroyed a human sense of balance. Karl Stern describes this contemporary
psychic phenomenon as a "Flight from Woman" and explains that, with
modern men and women "The very possibility of being in the least
dependent or protected, or even being loved, amounts to nothing less than a
phantasy of mutilation or destruction."[12]

Certainly, with Miss Amelia, the experience of having an operation for
kidney stones was an experience of mutilation. She seems to have been unable
to survive the experience of being totally helpless and dependent, unless she
could justify it in pragmatic, business-like terms. Thus she kept the kidney
stones and later has them set as ornaments in a watch chain for Cousin
Lymon. McCullers writes, "It had been a terrible experience, from the first
minute to the last, and all she had got out of it were those two little stones;
she was bound to set great store by them, or else admit to a mighty sorry
bargain." Miss Amelia, then, has real difficulty in justifying any experience
unless, that is, she can extract from it something practical and tangible,
preferably in the shape of a profit. And so that is why the café and love seem

doomed from the start. The pattern of pragmatism is too deeply entrenched for these people to sustain, for long, the experience of delight for its own sake.

Here each person has such a deep-seated fear of tenderness that he cannot admit his need of another without self-effacement, followed by hatred of the self and resentment of the needed one as well. Karl Stern describes this psychic phenomenon as "an undue emphasis on the technical and the rational, and a rejection of what for want of a better term we call 'feeling,' [which] go with a neurotic dread of receiving, a fear of tenderness and of protection, and are invariably associated with an original maternal conflict."[13] Now both Marvin Macy and Amelia Evans, and apparently Lymon too, have been deprived of the security of motherly love, and each of them has a real dread of receiving and an inability to show tenderness or love except at the price of self-abandonment.

With her father, himself described as a "solitary man," Amelia may have been, despite her six-foot-two-inch stature, known as "Little" but with everyone else she is the big one, the dominant force. Amelia is "like a man," then, not because she wears overalls and swamp boots, nor because she is six feet two inches tall (though McCullers does remark that Amelia's height is indeed "not natural for a woman"), nor even because Amelia settles her disputes with men by a wrestling match; Amelia is "like a man," instead, simply because of her insatiable need to dominate. The assumption here is that it is masculine to dominate, to force one's shape upon matter, whereas it is feminine to be receptive and malleable. In these terms, Miss Amelia is as masculine as Marvin Macy; for we learn that "with all things which could be made by the hands, Miss Amelia prospered." (p. 2) But also, that "It was only with people that Miss Amelia was not at ease. People, unless they are willy-nilly or very sick, cannot be taken into the hands and changed overnight to something more worthwhile and profitable. So that the only use that Miss Amelia had for other people was to make money out of them. And in this she succeeded." (p. 2) Unless they are sick, she deals with people only to make a profit (until, that is, the café opens). And she deals with sick people because they are malleable. With them she can achieve a symbiotic union which confirms her sense of power even more than litigations and profit-making do. Thus this fiercely materialistic woman need charge no fees for doctoring, for power is its own reward. Miss Amelia, however, is incapable of dealing with female complaints. At the mention of a female problem she reacts "like a great, shamed, dumb-tongued child;" she is then, as much as the cruelly phallic Marvin Macy, in flight from the feminine.

With the coming of Lymon and the opening of the café, of course, Miss Amelia tries to change, to become female. She still wears overalls and swamp boots, but on Sundays she now wears a dress. She is "not so quick to cheat her fellow man." She becomes more sociable and even takes Lymon into her confidence about "the most delicate and vital matters." But these matters are mostly details about her property—where she keeps bankbook, keys, and whisky barrels. Certainly she never confides in Lymon about her ten-day marriage to Marvin Macy.

Miss Amelia tries very hard to be open and tender, for she does love Lymon, but she simply does not know how to show that love. She gives him presents when he is cross, and she spoils him as a foolish mother does a child, but she is unable to maintain a reciprocal relationship with him. Instead she smothers him in a symbiotic relationship which must itself be the cause of his deep fear of death, for, as McCullers explains, "the lover is forever trying to strip bare his beloved."

Miss Amelia is then no more capable of manifesting a healthy femininity than Marvin Macy is. She is alternately hard and soft, but cannot manage to balance the qualities or to be both at once. She is, as McCullers explains, "divided between two emotions." Thus when Marvin Macy returns, she puts aside her overalls and wears always the dark red dress as symbol of her accessibility. She tries giving Marvin free drinks and smiling at him in a "wild, crooked way." But she also sets a terrible trap for him and tries to poison him. And she is no more successful at destroying him than she is at attracting him. She remains then the figure in the boarded-up house, white and sexless, the eyes turning increasingly inward upon themselves.

Amelia is left in the prison of her aloneness because the stereotyped patterns by which she encountered others were exclusively those of dominance or subjugation. She has known no way to love without self-abasement. Nor has Marvin Macy. Nor has Cousin Lymon. And self-abasement can only result in resentment and eventual retaliation, so Marvin Macy has his turn taking from Amelia and then, with Lymon's help, destroys the café in order to get his own back from her.

All these relationships are organically incomplete because no one knows how to give without vitiating his own integrity and no one knows how to take without enhancing his sense of personal power. These characters need to dismiss the sexual stereotypes of extremity and to learn to be strong without cruelty, tender without servility. The problem, then, is to reclaim the virtues of tenderness and receptivity from their exclusive association with whatever is female and weak, and to reinstate them as virtues which are essential to all humanity; for, without accepting these virtues as a dignified aspect of mankind, the human community cannot survive.

In a recent article entitled, "The Hard and the Soft: The Force of Feminism in Modern Times," Theodore Roszak quotes from the Tao Te Ching:

What is hard and stiff
Belongs to death;
The soft and tender belong to life.

The soft and tender, therefore, may not be excluded or rejected from life. Roszak's thesis is that "Saving the compassionate virtues is not the peculiar duty of women. On the contrary; the sooner we have done with the treacherous nonsense of believing that the human personality must be forced into masculine and feminine molds, the better."[14] The feminine virtues must not be rejected; they must be reclaimed by all humankind.

Once toward the end of McCullers' story, Marvin Macy laughs at Miss Amelia and says, "'Everything you holler at me bounces back on yourself.'" His denunciation provides an apt image for the entire novella. For *The Ballad of the Sad Café* may be interpreted as a fable which shows us that rejecting those characteristics labeled as exclusively feminine bounces back on the rejector and renders men and women alike incapable of loving and thereby escaping the prisons of their own spiritual isolation.

Now, we may have learned from contemporary cinema that we have "a failure to communicate" and from the popular song that "what the world needs now is luv, luv, luv," but only modern fiction has, to date, been subtle and serious enough to bring us to some understanding of why we have a communication gap and of how love can bridge that gap. In this tradition, McCullers' *Ballad* is especially significant; for to read it is to experience the solitude of the heart and to understand how misconceptions of love only reinforce that solitude.

NOTES

1. Alexis de Tocqueville, *Democracy in America*, II, ed. Phillips Bradley (New York: Alfred A. Knopf, 1963), p. 99.

2. Carson McCullers, "Preface" to *The Square Root of Wonderful* (Boston: Houghton Mifflin, 1958), p. viii.

3. Carson McCullers, *Collected Short Stories and the Novel, The Ballad of the Sad Café* (Boston: Houghton Mifflin, 1955). This edition is cited throughout this essay, with page references in the text.

4. D.H. Lawrence, "We Need One Another," *Phoenix: The Posthumous Papers of D.H. Lawrence*, ed. Edward D. McDonald (New York: The Viking Press, 1968), pp. 188–195.

5. The concept of the cheapness of human life recurs several times in McCullers' nonfiction as well. See *The Mortgaged Heart* (Boston: Houghton Mifflin, 1971), pp. 252, 254, and 281.

6. John B. Vickery, "Carson McCullers: A Map of Love," *Wisconsin Studies in Contemporary Literature*, I (Winter 1960), p. 15.

7. *The Mortgaged Heart*, p. 294.

8. Karl Stern, *The Flight from Woman* (New York: Noonday Press, 1970), p. 38.

9. *The Heart is a Lonely Hunter: The Novels and Stories of Carson McCullers* (New York: Houghton Mifflin, 1951), p. 273.

10. *The Mortgaged Heart*, p. 171.

11. See *The Art of Loving* (New York: Bantam Books, 1967), pp. 15–17.

12. Stern, p. 3.

13. *Ibid.*, p. 5.

14. Theodore Roszak, "The Hard and the Soft: The Force of Feminism in Modern Times," in *Masculine/Feminine: Readings in Sexual Mythology and the Liberation of Women*, ed. Betty Roszak and Theodore Roszak (New York: Harper and Row, 1969), p. 101.

MARGARET B. McDOWELL

The Ballad of the Sad Café *(1943)*

In *The Ballad of the Sad Café* McCullers achieved an intricate blending of the real and the mythic, of the comic and the desolate, and of the provincial and the universal. She attained in this short novel an extraordinary compression, control, objectivity, and sense of proportion. The narrative voice speaks at times in archaic diction and at times in a tone of leisured elegance; at still other times, in a pithy colloquial idiom. Though the three principal characters are grotesques, rather than fully-developed human beings and the villagers are not individualized, the "balladeer's" compassion for them pervades this book, as does his quiet humor when he pauses in the narrative to comment upon their inexplicable, eccentric, and often perverse behavior.

I A TURBULENT RELATIONSHIP

Kay Boyle declared *The Ballad of the Sad Café* a work in which an author "accepted the responsibility of being artisan as well as sensitive artist."[1] As in *Reflections in a Golden Eye*, McCullers attains in this novel an allegorical or "fairy-tale" exaggeration in her characters. Their freakishness, Boyle suggests, moves them beyond the range of ordinary human experience. Nevertheless, the thematic content of *The Ballad of the Sad Café* is not so remote as Boyle intimates from McCullers' personal life, her search for self-

From *Carson McCullers*. © 1980 by G.K. Hall & Co.

identification, and her exploration of unusual sexual experience. In creating intricate emotional diversities as characteristic of the life of Miss Amelia Evans, McCullers reflects, to a degree, the turbulence of her own life at the time she wrote this work, a turbulence emerging from the compounding of deep conflicts and complex relationships—the love and hate she felt for Reeves, whom she was divorcing; the strong, but frustrated, love she felt for her new friend Annemarie Clarac-Schwarzenbach; and the bewildering, but warm, affection she was discovering for David Diamond, who was attracted both to her and to Reeves. In *The Ballad of the Sad Café* McCullers assimilated all of these confused loves and disappointments when she conceived and almost completed the tale in the summer of 1941 at Yaddo and announced to Diamond that she would dedicate it to him.

The fact that *Reflections in a Golden Eye* was dedicated to Annemarie Clarac-Schwarzenbach in the summer of 1940 and *The Ballad of the Sad Café* to David Diamond the following summer suggests how fully McCullers had by this time confronted her bisexuality and that of her husband, who was during these months living with Diamond in New York. In this novel McCullers explores such themes as sexual ambivalence, destructive infatuation, the pain of being rejected by the beloved, the problematical configurations implied in any love triangle, and the paradoxical closeness of love and hate.

McCullers, hoping to return with renewed creativity to the uncompleted *The Bride* (later *The Member of the Wedding*), expected, for a time, to publish both of these short works in the same volume. However, the subtle balance of mood, theme, and image she sought in the story of Frankie Addams' adolescence continued to evade her until 1945. In the meantime, she published *The Ballad of the Sad Café* in *Harpers Bazaar*, August 1943.

Though Carson McCullers ostensibly used a southern mill town as setting for *The Ballad of the Sad Café*, the locale is also an imaginatively created milieu inhabited by grotesque and improbable characters—a milieu, for example, in which a female giant, Miss Amelia Evans, possesses, in the eyes of the villagers, awesome powers. As the tale opens and as it closes, life in the village is so static that "the soul rots with boredom" (65),[2] but for a short time between the opening of the story and its final sequence, the town becomes a place where strange and unbelievable events occur and where the three principal participants exist in some indefinable state between the human and the supernatural.

McCullers exhibits in this novel many of the properties of the ballad. Its plot is direct and swift; the action is familiar, rooted in folk tradition; and the language, stylized and intense, derives a quality of artifice from McCullers' studied use of archaic words and phrases. The narrator presents himself as a balladeer with much starkness of vision, an individual who establishes a desolate beginning and end for his tale, before he expands upon the intervening action, which he summarizes quickly in his opening words:

> The owner of the place was Miss Amelia Evans. But the person most responsible for the success and gaiety of the place was a hunchback called Cousin Lymon. One other person had a part in the story of this café—he was the former husband of Miss Amelia, a terrible character who returned to the town after a long term in the penitentiary, caused ruin, and then went on his way again. The café has long since been closed, but it is still remembered. (4)

Although he is responsible for the lively atmosphere in the café and provides his townsmen with food, drink, and fellowship, Lymon accentuates the sinister, as well as the comic, tone of the novel. One evening at dusk this dwarf hunchback trudges into the town and identifies himself as Miss Amelia's cousin. The villagers sitting on Miss Amelia's steps find him repulsive: "His hands were like dirty sparrow claws" (7). (McCullers, in fact, uses bird imagery throughout the novel to describe Lymon.) Because Miss Amelia thought that she had no relatives—a situation which sets her apart from other people—she is filled with wonder by the dwarf's insistent claim of kinship. She offers him a drink from the bottle in her overalls pocket "to liven his gizzard" (she owns the best still in the whole region), and she receives the weeping little man into her house.

Miss Amelia is a sorceress of reputation and establishes by her acts and attributes the ineffable atmosphere and eerie tone of the novel. She heals the diseases of the townfolk with her magical potions, and she regulates important events in their lives by telling them, for example, when the weather or the moon will be right for planting crops or for slaughtering hogs. Whenever her hated ex-husband, Marvin Macy, or her beloved dwarfed companion, Cousin Lymon, challenges her power and omniscience, the townspeople grow fearful and surly. While they respect her, they reveal curiosity and excitement about her, rather than deep concern. In their lack of affection, they become a vaguely malevolent force and, as it were, a sinister chorus to comment on the action. Consequently, when the townspeople do not see Lymon for the next three days, they assume that Amelia has murdered him. A self-appointed contingent arrives to investigate, and at this dramatic moment, Lymon makes a grand entrance from the top of the staircase, dressed in Amelia's fancy green shawl, which trails to the floor. He carries what the townsmen, astonished, recognize as the snuff box Amelia treasures because it belonged to her father. Lymon has filled it with cocoa and sugar, which he uses throughout the novel to sweeten his mouthful of decayed teeth.

McCullers' juxtaposition of past and present is notable. The narrator, soon after the opening sequence, moves back in time to reveal Amelia as she was at twenty, ten years before, when her father was still alive and cherished her. He had protected her, talked philosophically to her, and ridiculously nicknamed her "Little"; she slept calmly every night, as if covered with "warm axle grease." The narrator then dwells upon Amelia's present wealth, her ability to brew a liquor with magical properties, and her knowledge of folk medicine. Handsome enough to attract men, she is dark, tall, and muscular. She is a personage to be respected, not to be loved or pitied. Her chief recreation—bringing a lawsuit whenever she has a gambler's hunch that she may win it—suggests her selfishness and her shrewd eye for business.

A solitary individual, Amelia lacks any genuine basis for communication with either men or women. She has never cared for men, nor does she in this tale ever have a conversation with a woman; in fact, this book contains little direct conversation, the narrator more often summarizing the action. Amelia will not treat "female complaints," and blushes whenever talk of them arises. She also wears men's overalls. Though she denies her own femininity, she expresses maternal concern for children and is infinitely gentle in her treatment of them, making sure they are thoroughly anesthetized by drinking enough of her best liquor before she performs any painful operation.

Amelia's unconsummated marriage to Marvin Macy suggests that her denial of feminine identity may prevent her response to physical love from any man. In a large family of unwanted and abused children, Marvin Macy grew up with a stone in place of a heart, and as a young man he violated virgins throughout the land. Inexplicably, he falls in love with Amelia, reforms, and becomes suddenly humble. To the further astonishment of the townspeople, Amelia, soon after the death of her father, agrees to marry Macy. Awkward and uncomfortable in her wedding dress, Amelia amuses the guests as she reaches for the pockets of her overalls to rest her hands in them. In the days after the wedding, the mood of the villagers shifts dramatically from surprise and amusement to shock when they recognize that Amelia denies Macy access to her bedroom, abuses her lovesick groom, and finally orders him off her property.

If Amelia gains some sympathy at the beginning and the end of the book, at the point of her marriage she is almost monstrous, the female who preys upon the male whom she has lured to her abode. Though the townspeople react with disbelief to her humiliation of Macy, they also derive perverse pleasure from the fact that "someone has been thoroughly done in by some scandalous and terrible means" (31). They are tainted by the evil that Amelia herself seems to have let loose in the community.

Vengeance pervades the latter part of the tale when Macy returns to inflict vengeance upon the woman who has betrayed his love. In building toward the physical struggle between Amelia and Macy, which provides the climax for the book, the narrator slows the pace. About six years altogether pass between Lymon's appearance in town and his departure. Lymon immediately falls in love with Amelia's ex-husband and, because Macy does not accept this love, Lymon sits mourning on the porch rail, "like a bird on a telephone wire." Amelia must bury her pride and give Macy the best room in her house, to prevent Lymon's leaving with him. She concludes: "It is better to take in your mortal enemy than face the terror of living alone" (56).

Tension builds from August to Ground Hog Day, when the great confrontation takes place between Macy and Amelia, a struggle with overtones of the Grendel–Beowulf encounter. The townspeople are "recklessly glad" as they anticipate the battle between Amelia and Macy, a struggle of interminable length because of the mythical strength possessed by each antagonist. Only the intercession of the demonic Lymon, a still more powerfully mythical figure, finally defeats Amelia in the agonizingly protracted wrestling contest. A creature who vaguely possesses the characteristics of a pet, as well as human (or subhuman) attributes, Lymon now, like a hawk propelling himself through the air, leaps on Amelia's back, digs his birdlike claws into her shoulders, and helps to overcome her. Victorious after battle, Macy and Lymon steal Amelia's treasures and pillage her home and her still. Amelia waits three lonely years for Lymon to return at dusk before she boards up forever the windows of her dilapidated building. As at the beginning of the novel, the men of the prison chain gang can be heard singing as they work on the highway—twelve people who have escaped the solitary existence—but who are together only because they are in chains. Spontaneous and lasting fellowship is an impossibility in this novel. The forced and uneasy fellowship in the café, like the harmony and solidarity of the chain gang, lacks genuineness.

The novel is remarkable for its sweep over wide reaches of time while it also achieves much compression and concentration. Four years elapse between Part I, when Lymon arrives, and Part II when he and Amelia are seen operating the café and talking in the long evenings together. Two years elapse between Part II and Part III, when trouble settles in upon Amelia as Lymon falls in love with her enemy.

II GOTHIC, MYTHICAL, AND BALLAD ASPECTS OF THE NOVEL

McCullers claimed that in *The Ballad of the Sad Café* she tried to illustrate the superiority of Agapé (communal affection) over Eros (passionate love). Actually, the novel demonstrates the destructive nature of Eros in the lives of the three main characters, Miss Amelia Evans, Cousin Lymon, and Marvin Macy. McCullers' suggestion of Agapé is at best minimal, and appears only in the brief and uncertain pleasure the villagers enjoy at the café. Even more elusive than the fickle Eros, Agapé provides a joy to be savored in passing, rather than a durable influence through which one might shape a lifetime. The townspeople develop no continuing sense of community but remain easily frightened and suspicious of Amelia and Cousin Lymon. They rise to no significant realization of Agapé, even if the tenuous fellowship they find at the café provides a few moments of satisfaction in the meaningless repetition of their days. But perhaps Agapé does win out by implication, for it is surely superior to the destructiveness of Eros as it is dramatized in this book.

In demonstrating the destructive nature of Eros in the lives of Amelia, Macy, and Lymon, McCullers implies that any three-sided love affair, particularly a bisexual one, can be expected to fail, and, beyond this, most love affairs between two people will not endure.

McCullers' theme of the isolated individual seeking escape from loneliness through love, which had inspired *The Heart Is a Lonely Hunter*, became exceedingly complex by the time she wrote this third novel. In her first novel, she had presented loneliness as an affliction of the solitary "hunter," who may possibly be cured by love and certainly can be cured by nothing else. But she indicated even in that novel, through the other characters' attraction to Singer, that love is often mere narcissism and that any individual craves response from an admiring lover primarily to reinforce his or her self-esteem. Such characters want not so much to love as to be loved. Only Antonapoulos eludes Singer's love, and ironically only he is beloved by Singer. In McCullers' second novel, *Reflections in a Golden Eye*, lust rather than love dominates the vortex of sadism, masochism, self-pity, and violence so dramatically presented. In *The Ballad of the Sad Café* she again addressed the dominant theme of her first novel: the ambiguity in love. The beloved resents and fears the lover, though he also needs him and craves his presence. Love, because it reveals one's inmost identity, causes the lover and the beloved to be psychologically vulnerable to each other and even more accessible to betrayal by any third person who may gain access to their private world. In a forthright passage, the narrator acknowledges the inescapable power of such paradoxical attraction and repulsion: "There are the lover and the beloved, but these two come from different countries.... The beloved fears and hates the lover, and with the best of reasons. For the lover is forever trying to strip bare his beloved" (24–25).

Thus love becomes in this novel a force which drives the lover into deeper isolation by driving him in on himself. Love is the dreadful result of an individual's isolation and its intensifier, rather than its cure. Eros, if frustrated, leads to hatred and destruction; Agapé is an ideal, an inspiriting influence seldom to be attained as a pure and lasting force, though it alone can give order and meaning to our chaotic lives.

Because it embodies qualities of the gothic as McCullers defined them in "The Russian Realists and Southern Literature," *The Ballad of the Sad Café*, like *Reflections in a Golden Eye*, is interesting to consider as evidence that she herself turned rapidly toward the gothic mode after she wrote this essay. The kind of novel written in this mode, she continued, is antithetical to the meticulous and reportorial depiction of character and milieu which she found, perhaps mistakenly, typical of most contemporary Southern fiction. In her view, it was imprecise and simplistic to apply the term "gothic" to such complex works as William Faulkner's *As I Lay Dying* largely on the basis of their combination of beauty and the sinister and their juxtaposition of the comic and the tragic, although Faulkner's works contain elements of the gothic as she defined them and as she began to use them in her own work.

In her presentation of situation and characters in *The Ballad of the Sad Café*, McCullers herself dramatically blends realistic detail with romantic and supernatural elements. Like gothic novelists, as she defined them, she herself attains striking effects of ambivalence in her work through presenting Amelia's tragic betrayal by Lymon within a comic frame and through the use of everyday phrases, perhaps more typical of the comic mode, to convey the despair reflected in the latter part of the book.

Gothic fiction writers in England at the close of the eighteenth century maintained that fear distorts the perceptions of the psyche and that a phenomenon ordinarily discerned by the rational mind as trivial can become, under stress, momentarily overpowering both for the character and the reader. These early gothic authors often deliberately chose medieval settings, because they could thus embed their credulous characters in an age and milieu wherein unquestioning belief in miracles, visions, necromancy, and dreams was common. Such a world predisposes the characters to be sensitive to extrasensory perceptions and to see the normal as through a distorting lens. Frequently, these individuals confuse the probable with the improbable.

In *Reflections in a Golden Eye* McCullers localized the action by limiting it to a military base, in order to suggest the presence of a closed society. The characters are further enclosed by their lack of emotional and intellectual development. They are limited by their intense obsessions or "simple-mindedness." Their personal limitations and their narrowed environment predispose them to irrational fear when they are under pressure. Thus, even in writing *Reflections in a Golden Eye*, McCullers showed her understanding that fundamental to the gothic mode of fiction is the creation of psychic stress in the characters that will distort their perceptions and also will, in turn, communicate intimations of a psychic realm that transcends the ordinary.

By the time she produced *The Ballad of the Sad Café*, she thoroughly understood the "gothic" principle that irrational impulses of all sorts distort an individual's perception of reality. The result is that in extreme circumstances the character will find a trivial or harmless phenomenon overpowering. In both *Reflections in a Golden Eye* and *The Ballad of the Sad Café*, McCullers renders states of inner turmoil in terms of outward stress or in terms of the terrifying, the macabre, or the bizarre. Another aspect of traditional gothic fiction that now appealed to McCullers was the dramatization of forces of evil at large in the universe, beyond the control and understanding of the characters. Evil in both McCullers' second and third books appears as an unmotivated, irrational, or inexplicable phenomenon. She appreciated, furthermore, the power of such forces and probed their psychological effects on the individual more fully than did earlier romantic novelists exploring this mode. Her characters react irrationally in their frustrations or their anxiety and seem as fascinated by evil as repelled by it. She also assumes, as did many early gothic writers, that a close relationship exists between evil and human solitude or loneliness.

Although in McCullers' first novel Singer cannot survive his anguish, she emphasized the optimism of Mick Kelly and Portia Copeland in the face of suffering. In *Reflections in a Golden Eye* and in *The Ballad of the Sad Café* she recognized more decisively that irrationality and evil lie as close to the heart of human experience as do the hunger for love and its possible redemptive influence. Whoever acknowledges that the cosmos is malign (or even sees that it is indifferent to the individual human being) may learn to laugh at it, she felt, may also learn to accept the fact that life is strange, uncomfortable, and never fully meaningful in human and rational terms, and may further realize that effort and inertia are equally powerless to change the universe.

In *The Ballad of the Sad Café*, as in her first novel, the principal character remains a lonely hunter after a brief period of love expended upon an unlovable and unresponsive person. Pity for others and the desire to achieve a meaningful communion with them is absent, moreover, as the isolation in the lives of Amelia, Macy, and Lymon intensifies. In *The Ballad of the Sad Café* isolation, fear, and guilt also return to the lives of the townspeople after the struggle between Amelia and Macy leaves her defeated.

Even though McCullers in *The Ballad of the Sad Café* projects her characters more decidedly into a fantastic milieu than she did in *Reflections in a Golden Eye*, paradoxically the figures in *The Ballad of the Sad Café* emerge as more individualized figures and as people more often worthy of sympathy than those presented in the earlier book. In addition to being grotesques or eccentrics, Amelia, Lymon, and Macy sometimes reach universal and archetypal dimensions, as they reflect certain complexities in human relationships and the strong individual's insight into his or her own situation.

All the characters illustrate these challenging complexities. The giantlike Amelia, foolishly but lovingly nicknamed "Little" by her father, is, as an adult, afraid to assume her full sexual identity and remains his little child. Lymon, the hunchbacked dwarf, openly weeps for himself, longs for a male lover, and finds pleasure in inciting trouble among other individuals, but he also has a shrewd sense of the realities that encompass him. Of all the characters, Lymon's behavior is the least predictable; his motivation, the most paradoxical and ironic. He is both more and less than a man, neither adult nor child, neither sparrow and hawk nor quite human. Injured irreparably as a small child by poverty and by his parents' mistreatment, Macy, in his turn, regresses to rebellion, self-destruction, and vengefulness when he encounters rejection in his marriage; but he also elicits sympathy as a victim of forces which are too powerful for him to control. His behavior, likewise, is at times far from the ordinary, since he exists with only a stone where his heart had been; he cannot react in the usual human mode when his emotions are involved.

Amelia is also an unusual and complicated individual. In spite of the comic means used by McCullers to characterize her, she becomes a figure capable of deep and poignant suffering. She is the one who symbolizes most forcibly the inevitable isolation experienced by most persons—an isolation which may be the result of their self-centered behavior. She has been set apart at the beginning by the townspeople as a woman with special understandings and powers, and at the end she is isolated as one who, through a series of peculiar incidents and relationships, has been overcome by incomprehensible forces of evil.

Like the anonymous townspeople, the three chief characters, in spite of their legendary powers, are intense, irrational, superstitious, and naive. Amelia hides her uncertainty behind her shrewd business activity and her ability to take risks in her law suits, but even she is fearful of what she perceives as supernatural messages manifested in natural events or objects. The townspeople are childlike, simplistic, easily frightened by events or objects which they do not understand but also easily delighted by small pleasures, like the bright decorations in the café. Such lack of sophistication makes McCullers' presentation of them as superstitious and suspicious all the more credible. They are bound by long traditions of folk-knowledge, some of which are terrifying, some of which are amusing, and some of which provide colorful language and imagery for McCullers' tale.

The café becomes a joyous place where poor people, trapped in monotonous work in the textile mill, can see themselves as individuals of some worth; but this sense of worth grows in them only through the potency of Miss Amelia's liquor, which provides warmth and which also has the magical power to heal, to kill pain, and even to produce sexual potency. Amelia herself does not seem to know the exact significance of the acorn that she picked up the afternoon her father died when Cousin Lymon questions her about it, but the narrator hints that perhaps it symbolizes masculinity, her father's love, or his death. Likewise, the significance of the kidney stone removed from Amelia's body assumes special awesomeness for her, perhaps because it caused her the greatest pain she experienced before the agony of Lymon's desertion. Throughout the book, the villagers perceive various phenomena as mysterious portents. For example, the snowfall which bewilders Amelia, as well as the townsfolk, freezes her spirit into silence so that her speech sounds muffled—her aborted speech reflects her benumbed inner being. The snowfall is surely an omen, but one she cannot interpret to her satisfaction.

Most dramatic in its resemblance to folk legends which glorify the heroic is the climactic fight between Amelia and Macy, which achieves dimensions far beyond the natural and the ordinary. Bird imagery presages this struggle: "A hawk with a bloody breast flew over the town and circled twice around the property of Miss Amelia" (28). The conquest occurs on Ground Hog Day, a day of portent. Lymon early that morning takes a solitary journey into the swampland to see whether the animal sees his shadow, much as a character in mythology might sojourn into the netherworld to gain knowledge about his own fate and destiny. Because the weather is "neither rainy nor sunny but with a neutral temperature" (58), the groundhog casts an indeterminate image and so foreshadows the long impasse of the wrestling match. The deliberate, ceremonial decorum of the antagonists lends solemnity to the event: "They walked toward each other with no haste, their fists already gripped, and their eyes like the eyes of dreamers" (60–61). At one point, the narrator turns from the deadlocked belligerents to describe imperturbably the other spectators. When he finally returns to the match, he soberly exaggerates the length of time in which the struggle has hung in balance: "Perhaps it was half an hour before the course of the fight shifted. Hundreds of blows had been exchanged, and there was still a deadlock" (62). Little dramatic action occurs in the book except for this great event of extraordinary violence. Anticipation, memory, and long anxiety are far more important in creating intensity and ominousness than the incidents themselves.

As later in *The Member of the Wedding*, the frequent, unexplained, and incantatory repetition of the numbers *three* and *seven* suggests magical or religious ritual. The numbers appear in many connections. For three days and three nights after Lymon's arrival, the townspeople do not see him. Repeatedly, the narrator claims three good persons live in town, but their identity remains secret, as does that of the three persons who are said to come from Society City to see the fight. After her dramatic fight, Amelia knocks her fist on her desk three times and then begins to sob. Three years she waits for Lymon to return before boarding up her house. Her medicines may be efficacious because the number *seven* appears in the directions: seven swallows of water for hiccups, seven runs around the millpond for crick in the neck, and seven doses of Amelia's Miracle Mover for curing worms. Macy's cruelty derives from his upbringing as one of seven unwanted children. Seven times Amelia invites Lymon to go with her to Cheehaw, on the fateful day that he stays home alone, meets Macy, and falls in love with him. The townfolk know intuitively that the climactic and brutal struggle which forces Amelia to acknowledge Macy's mastery will take place at 7:00 that evening.

The attribution of magical properties to certain numbers occurs in folklore of many cultures. This ritualistic use of numbers suggests a universal significance to this tale that extends it far beyond the life of one woman in an obscure village. The narrator's archaic formality also hints at a wider significance in the story he tells.

The novel contains relatively little dialogue. Hence, the narrator's voice becomes particularly important in establishing shifts in tone or mood.[3] His acknowledgment of the efficacy of incantatory rhythms in the repetition of certain numbers reflects his willingness to share the superstitions of the naive villagers. He thus gives credence to the villagers' beliefs, and he himself seems to believe in the gossip that they pass about, exaggerated and malicious as it may be. The narrator shifts unpredictably from using the voice of a laborer at the mill, talking after work with an audience of other bored mill hands, to using the voice of a mystical balladeer who speaks in a poetic, archaic, and stylized pattern. The balladeer's omniscience and his primitive sensibility seem inconsistent with the colloquial voice of the millworker, though they both ultimately reveal a folk origin. As poetic singer, he remarks, for instance, that Macy upon his return from prison "caused ruin" (4). But the colloquial idiom, comic in its emphasis, dominates most of the narrative passages. The humor in them gains much of its ludicrous effect from a colorful vocabulary, a curious phrasing, or a use of surprising illustrations. In his simple and direct sentences, the narrator, on the other hand, often eloquently expresses his philosophy as oracular wisdom. He moves in a moment from the comic to the profound.

The contrast between the comic idiom and the poetic expression in the narrative voice may be illustrated in the descriptions of Amelia's wonderful brew. When her liquor is not available, the narrator complains sadly that all other whiskey in the region is of such poor quality that "those who drink it grow warts on their liver the size of goobers" (63). In contrast to such colloquial comic imagery, the narrator elsewhere describes Amelia's liquor in highly poetic context. For instance, it can make the spinner or weaver, whose sensitivity is long dulled by monotonous work, take a marsh lily in the palm of his hand and discover in it a significance that warms his soul. As an invisible message written in lemon juice becomes visible when held under the warmth of a lamp, so the mysteries of the universe, the narrator asserts, can be seen through the magical warmth of Amelia's brew. Her liquor opens astonishing worlds to the townspeople. Beyond "the loom, the dinner pail, the bed and then the loom again," a man can "see for the first time the cold, weird radiance of a midnight January sky, and a deep fright at his own smallness stops his heart" (9–10).

In addition to the narrator's continual shifting between the colloquial and the formal or poetic, his style is characterized throughout the book by an extensive use of lists, as if his credibility could best be increased by piling up factual details. After the climactic fight, for example, the narrator takes time to itemize the damage done to Amelia's property by Lymon and Macy. Whenever a meal is eaten, the narrator lists the menu, which includes the regional favorites: "fried chicken ... mashed rootabeggars, collard greens, and hot pale golden sweet potatoes" (10). He lists the names of all the eight men who call on Amelia early in the story to investigate the rumor that she has murdered Lymon, although we hear of none of them elsewhere in the tale. (Some of the details in these lists may be humorously irrelevant to the rest of the items in the series, a comic device used by McCullers in *Reflections in a Golden Eye*.)

The explicitness by which the narrator establishes Amelia's milieu helps him gain credence for Amelia as an inhabitor of that milieu and as an extraordinary personage. Though the exact sources of her remarkable power remain mysterious, that power is so carefully demonstrated and her fabulous reputation is so convincingly documented that one cannot question the validity of her legendary accomplishments. The narrator always presents her behavior, her feelings, her thoughts, her appearance, and her words concretely rather than in the abstract. For instance, instead of remarking that

Amelia was energetic and extremely busy in the autumn before Macy's return, the narrator recites a long series of her activities, comic in its specificity and variety:

> She made a new and bigger condenser for her still, and in one week ran off enough liquor to souse the whole country. Her old mule was dizzy from grinding so much sorghum, and she scalded her Mason jars and put away pear preserves.... She had traded for three tremendous hogs, and intended to make much barbecue, chitterlins, and sausage.... One day she sat down to her typewriter and wrote a story—a story in which there were foreigners, trap doors, and millions of dollars. (42)

Such a passage, with its celebration of a woman possessing remarkable vitality and zest, renders more poignant the effect of both the first and the last pages of this work, wherein the languor of life in the late summer afternoon town dominates. The narrator closes the tale, as he began it, by commenting quietly upon the twelve men on the chain gang, who represent, in part, the dull existence and the tragic boredom that ordinarily prevail in this town. As they sing, they leave behind them, for the moment, their misery. They begin to work in the early dawn. The ordinary daily routine of hard work and a suggestion of the eerie in their music—sounds which seem to emanate from both earth and air—contrast strangely, as do the black sky and the streaks of the golden sunrise and the skin of the black men and white. Disaster in their lives and peacefulness in their monotonous activity find expression in this "music intricately blended, both somber and joyful" (66).

Even more a prisoner now than these men, Amelia exists as an idle and remote presence behind the shutters of the dilapidated house on the now deserted street. At the close, she thus becomes more abstract, a mythic figure representing the deep, chronic isolation—which McCullers saw at the center of human life. Her face, dimly peering out from the darkness, is "sexless" because loneliness surrounds men and women alike. Because the most isolated people may become almost invisible, her face is like "the terrible dim faces" one sees only in dreams.

NOTES

1. "I Wish I Had Written *The Ballad of the Sad Café*," in *I Wish I Had Written That*, ed. Eugene J. Woods (New York, 1946), pp. 300–301.

2. Page numbers in parentheses in this chapter refer to *The Ballad of the Sad Café: The Novels and Stories of Carson McCullers* (Boston, 1951).

3. For further comment on the narrator as related to the mythic quality of the book,

see Dawson F. Gaillard, "The Presence of the Narrator in Carson McCullers' *The Ballad of the Sad Café*," *Mississippi Quarterly*, 25 (Fall 1972), 419–27; and Albert Griffith, "Carson McCullers' Myth of the Sad Café," *Georgia Review*, 21 (Spring 1967), 46–56. Also related to the mythic quality of the book is emphasis on the ballad form in the interpretation of the novel, as in Joseph. Millichap, "Carson McCullers' Literary Ballad," *Georgia Review*, 27 (Fall 1973), 329–39. The need for interpretation of this work in terms of its characteristics as a lyrical ballad with mythic implications may account for the negative reactions to Edward Albee's stage play based on the book. Cousin Lymon, in particular, could not be transferred to the stage without losing the sense of mystery and myth that surround him in the book.

Carson McCullers' Amazon Nightmare

Miss Amelia Evans is a monster creature, really, and yet Carson McCullers lavished admiring care in picturing her many talents, her forbidding strength, and her control of the squalid village world of *The Ballad of the Sad Café* (1943). Despite a good bit of critical attention to the novella and recent feminist interest in androgynous characters in literature, Miss Amelia's freakishness has not been seriously examined. It is crucial to the meaning of this grotesque fable, relating it closely to *The Heart Is a Lonely Hunter* and *The Member of the Wedding*. McCullers said that "Love, and especially love of a person who is incapable of returning or receiving it, is at the heart of my selection of grotesque figures to write about—people whose physical incapacity is a symbol of their spiritual incapacity to love or receive love—their spiritual isolation."[1] But Miss Amelia's peculiarities are more specific than mere "spiritual incapacity"; they reflect McCullers' ambivalence about female identity. Miss Amelia is a grown-up tomboy whose physical proportions symbolize her exaggerated masculine self-image.

Louis Rubin is perceptive in suggesting that McCullers destroys Mick Kelley and Frankie Addams as characters when she tries to force them beyond the pain of adolescent sexual awakening into an acceptance of womanhood.[2] She cannot really imagine such acceptance because she never found it herself. Friends often commented on her childlike manner, and her

From *Modern Fiction Studies* 28, no 3 (Autumn 1982). © 1982 by the Purdue Research Foundation.

adult photos present images of the same kind of fierce boyishness she described in both Mick and Frankie.[3] Virginia Spencer Carr's biography amply documents the sexual ambivalence revealed most explicitly in McCullers' declaration to Nelson Algren, "I was born a man."[4] It is this identification with the masculine that stimulates her imagination to explore the dangerous psychological territory of *The Ballad of the Sad Café*.

One critic calls McCullers' flat, childlike narrative tone "a kind of buffer to fend off what would otherwise be unbearable,"[5] but I would instead describe it as a strategy for placing the action at a safe enough remove from ordinary life to allow forbidden impulses free scope—at least for awhile. The form of *The Ballad of the Sad Café* allows McCullers to indulge the impulse to appropriate male power and thus escape the culturally inferior role of woman. There can be no other explanation for Miss Amelia's strapping physique, her skill at masculine trades, or her rejection of everything female, most apparent in her indignant refusal to play the physical part of a woman in her ten-day marriage to Marvin Macy. Her later relationship with Cousin Lymon is never threatening because he is not a real man who sees her as female. Behind the dream of independence represented by Miss Amelia's "masculinity," however, lies the fear of male vengeance which triumphs in the story's conclusion, as Marvin Macy and Cousin Lymon join forces to destroy the usurper. The formerly invincible Amazon is left shrunken and imprisoned in the slowly collapsing shell of her once prosperous café.

The folk tale atmosphere of *The Ballad of the Sad Café* may owe something to Isak Dinesen's *Seven Gothic Tales* (1934), whose strange ambience Carson McCullers never ceased to praise after a first reading in 1938.[6] Dinesen's work remained very close to her, and it is quite understandable that three years later, while she struggled to resolve Frankie Addams' anxiety about growing too tall, she might have remembered Dinesen's portrait of six-foot Athena Hopballehus in "The Monkey." Probably this process was not conscious; her imagination simply revived the motif of the Amazon in order to explore for herself some of the problems of sexual identity and female independence which Dinesen treats in her exotic fable. Robert S. Phillips was the first to comment on the similarities between *The Ballad of the Sad Café* and "The Monkey,"[7] but I think he overstates their extent. The only clear parallels are the motifs of the Amazon and her bitter hand-to-hand combat with a hated male suitor. These motifs are developed in very different ways by the two writers, and the stories move through entirely different atmospheres to almost opposite conclusions about the sources of female autonomy. Because McCullers' novella is a kind of challenge to the arguments implied by Dinesen's story, it is useful to remind ourselves of the significance of the Amazon maiden in "The Monkey."

The fairy tale world of "The Monkey" is centered in the female dominion of Cloister Seven, a wealthy retreat for unmarried ladies and widows of noble birth. It is ruled by a virgin Prioress with mysterious powers who resembles a sybil, the Chinese goddess Kuan-Yin, and the Wendish goddess of love. To all of the Cloister's inhabitants it is "a fundamental article of faith that woman's loveliness and charm, which they themselves represented in their own sphere and according to their gifts, must constitute the highest inspiration and prize of life."

Athena Hopballehus embodies this ideal femininity in heroic form. She is a motherless only child who has been raised by her father in a nearby castle, surrounded by "an atmosphere of incense burnt to woman's loveliness." The father admits, however, that "she has been to me *both* son and daughter, and I have in my mind seen her wearing the old coats of armor of Hopballehus" (my italics). The problem implied in this reference to androgynous childhood training is never explored in the story, but perhaps it is meant to suggest an excess of independence. At eighteen, Athena is six feet tall, powerful and broad-shouldered, with flaming red hair and the eyes of a young lioness or eagle. Athena is what her name suggests, a human type of the warrior goddess, whom Dinesen also associates with the virgin huntress Diana and "a giant's daughter who unwittingly breaks men when she plays with them." When a proposal of marriage is made by a handsome young cavalry officer named Boris, the Prioress' nephew and Athena's childhood playmate, Athena's fierce autonomy sparks an indignant refusal.

Although forceful womanhood dominates the world of "The Monkey," the story's central problem is not Athena's fate but rather the decadent weakness of the Prioress' nephew Boris. This overcultivated young man is the central consciousness of the narrative, and the plot follows his reluctant entrance into normal manhood through the manipulations of his aunt. The old ladies of Cloister Seven, having heard rumors of Boris' implication in a homosexual scandal, give him an ambiguous welcome when he arrives from the capital city. They think of him as "a young priest of black magic, still within hope of conversion." A sort of conversion is indeed accomplished by the end of the story, but only because the Prioress uses deception and magic to force the resisting bride and groom together. Threatening Boris by revealing her knowledge of the scandal, she induces him to drink a love potion and to force himself upon Athena. The maiden responds with her fist and knocks out two of his teeth. Dinesen tells us that all the young women Boris had previously rejected "would have felt the pride of their sex satisfied in the contemplation of his mortal pursuit of this maiden who now strove less to escape than to kill him." A fierce battle ensues, and she is about to dispatch him with a death grip on his throat when he transforms the nature of the conflict by forcing his mouth against hers. Instantly her whole body registers the terrible effect of his kiss. "As if he had run a rapier straight through her, the blood sank from her face, her body stiffened in his arms," her strength dissolved away, and she collapsed. Both Boris' and Athena's faces express "a deadly disgust" with the kiss.

In her ability to overcome even this revulsion, the Prioress emerges as the very incarnation of the Wendish goddess of love, half-monkey and half-human. Because Boris and Athena witness the Prioress' grotesque exchange of shapes with her monkey on the morning after the seduction attempt, they are united as initiates to the mystery of her power. They submit to her insistence that the sexes cannot remain separate; Boris must pay homage to female power, and the proud young Athena must renounce her heroic virginity in an alliance with him.

No union of male and female, however reluctant, occurs in *The Ballad of the Sad Café*. In contrast to Athena's essentially female power, Miss Amelia's remarkable strength depends on her masculinity in a world devoid of feminine qualities. All the characters who have speaking parts are males, except for Miss Amelia, who never betrays even a hint of conventionally feminine behavior.

Like Dinesen's Athena, Miss Amelia is a motherless only child raised by an adoring father, but McCullers gives her Amazon a more exaggerated physique and a mysterious authority. At the height of her adult pride, Miss Amelia is the central personality of her town. An imposing figure, she is "a dark, tall woman with bones and muscles like a man," hairy thighs, and short-cropped hair brushed back from her forehead like Mick Kelley's and Frankie Addams'. In the building she inherited from her father, she operates a profitable general store which gradually becomes the town's only café. She produces the best liquor in the county from her secret still in a nearby swamp; sells chitterlins, sausage, and golden sorghum molasses; owns farms in the vicinity; and is adept at all manual skills, such as carpentry, masonry, and butchery. The most impressive of all her powers, however, and the one that with the magical properties of her whiskey best reveals her nearly supernatural dimensions, is her ability to heal the sick. Like a sorceress or witch, she brews her own secret remedies from roots and herbs. "In the face of the most dangerous and extraordinary treatment she did not hesitate, and no disease was so terrible but what she would undertake to cure it."

There is one notable exception to Miss Amelia's healing powers:

If a patient came with a female complaint she could do nothing. Indeed at the mere mention of the words her face would slowly darken with shame, and she would stand there craning her neck against the collar of her shirt, or rubbing her swamp boots together, for all the world like a great, shamed, dumb-tongued child.

Her embarrassed confusion is a natural consequence of her total identification with masculinity and her childlike sexual innocence. Even in adulthood, Miss Amelia preserves the tomboy attitudes we encounter in Mick Kelley and Frankie Addams. For all of these characters, the first physical encounters with men are unpleasant surprises. We remember Mick's distaste for her one experience of lovemaking with Harry Minowitz and Frankie's terrified escape from the soldier who tried to seduce her. For both Mick and Frankie, sexual experience brought the necessary renunciation of childhood boyish freedom and a reluctant acceptance of adult femininity. But Miss Amelia refuses to accept the diminished status of woman. When she rather absentmindedly marries Marvin Macy, the whole town is relieved, expecting marriage to soften her character and physique "and to change her at last into a calculable woman." Instead, after the bridegroom follows her upstairs to bed on their wedding night, Miss Amelia stamps downstairs in a rage, wearing breeches and a khaki jacket. Until dawn she reads the Farmer's Almanac, smokes her father's pipe, and practices on her new typewriter. During the ensuing ten days of the abortive marriage, she sleeps downstairs and continues to ignore her husband unless he comes within striking range, when she socks him with her fist. Macy disappears from town in disgrace, leaving Amelia victorious in her Amazon virginity.

For ten uneventful years Miss Amelia goes about her solitary life, aloof, stingy, maintaining her strange control of the town. Then one night the little hunchbacked Cousin Lymon mysteriously appears on her doorstep, wins her heart, and causes momentous changes both in her life and in the life of the town for six years before the sinister return of Marvin Macy. The question is why Miss Amelia should have rejected a vigorous normal man, only to fall in love with a twisted midget. Joseph Millichap sees traditional folk tale elements in the characters of Marvin Macy and Cousin Lymon: Macy is a sort of demon lover, and Cousin Lymon is reminiscent of the figures of mysterious stranger and elf. But Millichap comes closer to answering our question when he says that Cousin Lymon "is a man loved without sex, a child acquired without pain, and a companion which her [Amelia's] limited personality finds more acceptable than a husband or a child."[8] Marvin Macy had been sufficiently ennobled by his love for Miss Amelia so that he might have been a tolerable mate for her, but, by accepting her feminine part in the marriage, Amelia would have had to renounce the masculine sources of her strength. Such a capitulation to the female mysteries that she has avoided all her life would be unthinkable. Her enraged reaction to Macy's forlorn attempts at lovemaking clearly expresses the insult they represent to her pride. Cousin Lymon, on the other hand, represents no threat to her power. He is a sickly, deformed mannikin whom she could crush with one blow of her fist, and, from all we can see, he makes no sexual demands. His warped, childlike form clearly indicates his masculine impotence, just as Amelia's grotesquely masculine appearance expresses her inability to function as a woman. With Lymon she feels safe in revealing affection, for she can baby and pet him without any threat of sexuality.

At the heart of Miss Amelia's relationship with Cousin Lymon, there is actually an inversion of traditional roles of male and female. Miss Amelia is physically dominant and provides a living for the household as a husband would. Cousin Lymon is the pampered mate who struts about in finery, is finicky about food and accommodations, and gads about town socializing and gossiping. He functions as a hostess would in the café, while Miss Amelia stands aloof and silent in the background. In their intimate conversations before the parlor fire, Miss Amelia sits with her "long legs stretched out before the hearth" contemplating philosophical problems and reminiscing about her father, while Cousin Lymon sits wrapped in a blanket or green shawl on a low chair and chatters endlessly about petty details.

Despite his physical weakness and his vanity, Cousin Lymon seems to embody the spirit of spring and renewal. He has drifted mysteriously into town in April, in a year when the crops promise well and conditions at the local mill are relatively prosperous. Once accepted as Miss Amelia's intimate, he becomes a catalyst for the release of her genial impulses. Her devotion to him brightens her face and gradually engenders a hospitality she had never expressed before. Before the hunchback's arrival, she sold her moonshine by the bottle, handing it out through her back door in the dark. Never was anyone allowed to open or to drink this liquor inside the building. But once Cousin Lymon is installed in her house, she begins selling it inside, providing glasses and plates of crackers for consumption on the premises. Gradually the store is transformed into a café with tables where Miss Amelia sells liquor by the drink and serves fried catfish suppers for fifteen cents a plate. Miss Amelia grows more sociable and less inclined to cheat her business associates. Even her special powers for healing and for brewing her marvelous liquor are enhanced. All these positive developments of her character expand themselves in the communal warmth which her café comes to provide for the town.

Though Cousin Lymon brings fruitful changes in the lives of Miss Amelia and her town, his own physical state suggests a fatal limitation to prosperity. He remains "weakly and deformed" despite Amelia's pampering and the exercise of her fullest healing abilities. He is also personally malicious, even though he has generally served as an agent for gaiety and warmth. Thus he is naturally drawn to the cruel strength of Marvin Macy, a force which complements his own unpleasant traits. When Macy suddenly returns to town from years in the state penitentiary, Cousin Lymon is immediately infatuated.

Macy embodies all the qualities of "normal" masculinity, but McCullers has cast them in an evil, destructive light throughout the story. Macy may be tall, brawny, and good-looking, but he is also violent and viciously lustful. He is the devil male who mutilates animals for fun and has ruined the tenderest young girls in the region. Amelia refers to Macy's cloven hoof, and the Satanic is also suggested by his red shirt and the fact that he never sweats. Throughout the story he is allied with winter. Even though he had been temporarily reformed by his love for Miss Amelia, their wedding took place on a winter day rather than in the traditionally propitious season of spring or of summer. His revengeful return to town sixteen years later comes in autumn and brings sinister portents of unseasonable weather, ruining the normally festive ritual of hog-butchering: "there was everywhere the smell of slowly spoiling meat, and an atmosphere of dreary waste." Macy lays claim to the unprecedented snowfall in January that gives the town "a drawn, bleak look." The climactic battle between Miss Amelia and Marvin Macy occurs exactly one month later, on ground-hog day. Its issue is foreordained by Cousin Lymon's report that the groundhog has seen its shadow and, therefore, that more winter lies ahead.

Understanding at once that Macy's return to town is a challenge, Miss Amelia begins preparations for a fight, taunting Macy by wearing her red dress as a flagrant reminder of his failure to make her act the part of a woman during their marriage.[9] While she wears the dress, she pokes her biceps constantly, practices lifting heavy objects, and works out with a punching bag in her yard. In the climactic battle between the two antagonists, the question to be decided is not, as in Dinesen, whether a powerful young woman can be subdued so that a union of the sexes can occur. For McCullers, the contest will decide whether a woman can deny her sex and dominate men with a strength analogous to their own.

> Now the test had come, and in these moments of terrible effort, it was Miss Amelia who was the stronger. Marvin Macy was greased and slippery, tricky to grasp, but she was stronger. Gradually she bent him over backward, and inch by inch she forced him to the floor.... At last she had him down, and straddled; her strong big hands were on his throat.

Suddenly, at this moment of Miss Amelia's triumph, Cousin Lymon leaps across the room from his perch on the bar to aid his adored male friend. He lands on Amelia's back and changes the balance of force to Macy's advantage. Miss Amelia is destroyed.

The sexual dynamics of *The Ballad of the Sad Café* are an inversion of traditional heterosexual patterns. Contrasts with Dinesen's "The Monkey" help reveal the masculine sources of Miss Amelia's autonomous strength and point up McCullers' complete rejection of heterosexual union. Rather than accepting her femininity by consummating her marriage to the aggressively masculine Marvin Macy, Miss Amelia focuses her affections on the little hunchback who seems to function simultaneously as child, pet, and rather feminine companion. But Cousin Lymon is much less devoted to Miss Amelia than she is to him, and this gives him an emotional advantage over her which proves ultimately disastrous. It seems inevitable that the foppish dwarf should fall helplessly in love with Marvin Macy, thus completing the destructive triangular relationship which McCullers used to develop her theory that "almost everyone wants to be the lover" and that "in a deep secret way, the state of being loved is intolerable to many." But this theory and McCullers' statement that *Ballad* was intended to show the inferiority of passionate individual love to *agape*[10] fail to account for the individual peculiarities of her characters and for the sexual dimensions of their problems in love. The real force of *The Ballad of the Sad Café* lies in its depiction of a masculine Amazon whose transgression of conventional sexual boundaries brings catastrophic male retribution. Unlike Dinesen, who portrayed an uneasy compromise between proud female autonomy and reluctant masculine homage, McCullers sought to deny the feminine entirely and to allow a woman to function successfully as a man. She could not sustain her vision because she knew it was impossible. I believe that the consequences of her experiment in this novella play a part in determining the final form of *The Member of the Wedding*, which, as I have argued elsewhere,[11] inexorably moves Frankie toward an acceptance of conventional femininity. After writing *The Ballad of the Sad Café* in only a few months, when McCullers returned to her six-year struggle with the materials of *The Member of the Wedding*, she knew that Frankie would have to submit as Miss Amelia had not.

NOTES

1. *The Mortgaged Heart*, ed. Margarita C. Smith (Boston, MA: Houghton Mifflin, 1971), p. 274.

2. "Carson McCullers: The Aesthetic of Pain," *Virginia Quarterly Review*, 53 (1977), 278–279.

3. See, for example, Virginia Spencer Carr, *The Lonely Hunter* (Garden City, NY: Anchor Books, 1976), plates 7–9, 22, 28, 30, and 34.

4. Carr, pp. 110, 112, 125, 129, and 159.

5. Robert Rechnitz, "The Failure of Love: The Grotesque in Two Novels by Carson McCullers," *Georgia Review*, 22 (1968), 460.

6. *The Mortgaged Heart*, pp. 269–270.

7. "Dinesen's 'Monkey' and McCullers's 'Ballad': A Study in Literary Affinity," *Studies in Short Fiction*, 1 (1963–1964), 184–190. Phillips sees both stories in Freudian terms of father–daughter incest that renders the daughter unfit for normal heterosexual love. Carolyn Heilbrun suggests another possibility in *Reinventing Womanhood* (New York: Norton, 1979), p. 107. Heilbrun sees identification with the masculine as typical of girls who grow up to be achievers in business and professional life. By rejecting the mother and modeling herself on the dominant parent who seems to act as a free agent in the larger world, the child denies the conventional female destiny of submission and entrapment. Miss Amelia can be seen as a fictional example of this pattern. Her identification with Big Papa is made convenient by the complete absence of any female force in her upbringing.

8. "Carson McCullers's Literary Ballad," *Georgia Review*, 27 (1973), 334–335.

9. Reid Broughton, in "Rejection of the Feminine in Carson McCullers's *The Ballad of the Sad Café*," *Twentieth Century Literature*, 20 (1974), 34–43, argues that the dress is a symbol of Amelia's accessibility, but that interpretation is denied by all her behavior. Rechnitz, p. 461, thinks she is trying to lure Macy away from Cousin Lymon, but, again, her behavior is the opposite of seductive.

10. *The Mortgaged Heart*, pp. 280–281.

11. "Carson McCullers's *Tomboys*," *Southern Humanities Review*, 14 (1980), 339–350.

MARY ANN DAZEY

Two Voices of the Single Narrator in The Ballad of the Sad Café

When *The Ballad of the Sad Café* was first published in *Harper's Bazaar* in 1943, Carson McCullers was twenty-six, and at that time most critics pointed to the work as evidence of the great promise of the young writer. Today, however, it is ranked along with *The Member of the Wedding* as her most successful work. McCullers' choosing to call the sad, romantic tale a ballad has caused many to discuss her ballad style in some fashion. In his work *Carson McCullers*, Lawrence Graver, for example, concludes that *The Ballad of the Sad Café* is one of her most "rewarding works" in part because she employed "a relaxed colloquial style, punctuating the narrative with phrases like 'time must pass' and 'so do not forget.'"[1] Ironically, Dayton Kohler, eighteen years earlier, had selected these identical lines as evidence of McCullers' "stylistic coyness," which he called "poetically false and out of the context with the objective drama." He further determined that the passages where the narrator stops the flow of the story to make "wise observations" indicate McCullers' own feelings that her story was "too weak to carry unsupported its burden of theme and sensibility."[2] Both critics are reacting to what Dawson F. Gaillard determines is the changing voice of the narrator. Gaillard points out that in the first paragraph of the story, for example, the narrator's voice is "flat" and "inflectionless" and is "adjusted" to

From *The Southern Literary Journal* 17, no. 2 (Spring 1985). © 1985 by the Department of English of the University of North Carolina at Chapel Hill.

the "dreariness" of the town; then it changes and loses the flatness to become the ballad teller.[3] This ballad maker, Joseph R. Millichap concludes, "fixes the style of the novel." His voice permits McCullers to weave her literary ballad into a perfect blend of the "literate and colloquial."[4]

A stylistic analysis of *The Ballad of the Sad Café* reveals that McCullers has created a single narrator with two distinctly different voices. In the first voice the narrator places the characters and their actions in the mainstream of human existence. This voice begins, "The town itself is dreary"[5] and ends, "Yes, the town is dreary" (p. 70). This voice concludes the introduction, "You might as well walk down to the Forks Falls Road and listen to the chain gang" (p. 4) and ends the story, "You might as well go down to the Forks Falls highway and listen to the chain gang" (p. 71). Not only does this voice provide the frame for the drama, but it also flows throughout the story as a second voice of the single narrator. In this voice the reader is sometimes addressed directly and even commanded to respond to the narration.

For the voice of the ballad maker, who actually tells the tale of Miss Amelia, her ten-day bridegroom, and her cousin Lymon, McCullers chooses past tense verb forms. When the first voice, the voice of the lamenter, encountered at the beginning of the novel, speaks, McCullers chooses present tense verb forms. The first shift occurs after Cousin Lymon has appeared and has been offered a drink of Miss Amelia's whiskey. The narrator explains:

> The whiskey they drank that evening (two big bottles of it) is important. Otherwise, it would be hard to account for what followed. Perhaps without it there would never have been a café. For the liquor of Miss Amelia has a special quality of its own. It is clean and sharp on the tongue, but once down a man it glows inside him for a long time afterward. And that is not all. It is known that if a message is written with lemon juice on a clean sheet of paper there will be no sign of it. But if the paper is held for a moment to the fire then the letters turn brown and the meaning becomes clear. (p. 10)

Next this voice draws the reader into the experience, and McCullers employs the first of eight imperatives that run throughout the first half of the novel (italics in quotations mine):

> *Imagine* that the whiskey is the fire and that the message is that which is known only in the soul of a man—then the worth of Miss Amelia's liquor can be understood. Things that have gone

unnoticed, thoughts that have been harbored far back in the dark mind are suddenly recognized and comprehended. (p. 10)

The second of the eight imperatives occurs after the regular group of townsmen has been named and described. The ballad maker says, "Each of them worked in the mill, and lived with others in a two- or three-room house for which the rent was ten dollars or twelve dollars a month. All had been paid that afternoon, for it was Saturday." And the lamenting voice adds, "So, for the present, *think* of them as a whole" (p. 20).

In the third imperative, the narrator becomes a camera which provides a long shot of Miss Amelia and Cousin Lymon as the two establish a pattern of behavior over the years:

> So for the moment *regard* these years from random and disjointed views. *See* the hunchback marching in Miss Amelia's footsteps when on a red winter morning they set out for the pinewoods to hunt. *See* them working on her properties—with Cousin Lymon standing by and doing absolutely nothing, but quick to point out any laziness among the hands. On autumn afternoons they sat on the back steps chopping sugar cane. The glaring summer days they spent back in the swamp where the water cypress is a deep black green, where beneath the tangled swamp trees there is a drowsy gloom. When the path leads through a bog or a stretch of blackened water *see* Miss Amelia bend down to let Cousin Lymon scramble on her back—and *see* her wading forward with the hunchback settled on her shoulders, clinging to her ears or to her broad forehead.

* * *

> For the hunchback was sickly at night and dreaded to lie looking into the dark. He had a deep fear of death. And Miss Amelia would not leave him by himself to suffer with this fright. It may even be reasoned that the growth of the café came about mainly on this account; it was a thing that brought him through the night. So *compose* from such flashes an image of these years as a whole. And for a moment *let* it rest. (pp. 24–25).

The next imperative instructs the reader in his understanding of Miss Amelia's peculiar behavior and prepares him for the story of Marvin Macy and Miss Amelia's ten-day marriage: "*Remember* that it all happened long ago, and that it was Miss Amelia's only personal contact, before the hunchback came to her, with this phenomenon—love" (p. 27). And at the end of the recital of events concerning the brief marriage and Marvin Macy's departure from town, this voice again addresses the reader, "So *do* not *forget* this Marvin Macy, as he is to act a terrible part in the story which is yet to come" (p. 34). The final instructions to the reader are delivered when Marvin Macy is about to return to town and change the lives of Miss Amelia and Cousin Lymon forever: "So *let* the slow years pass and come to a Saturday evening six years after the time when Cousin Lymon came first to the town" (p. 38).

Constantly flowing alongside these imperatives and the lively voice of the ballad maker are the generalizations made by the lamenting voice about the specific actions of the characters. The specific action of a character is told in past tense, but the interpretation is always in the present tense. Of Cousin Lymon, the subjective narrator explains, "There is a type of person who *has* a quality about him that sets him apart from other and more ordinary human beings. Such a person *has* an instinct to establish immediate and vital contact between himself and all things in the world." And the ballad maker observes, "Certainly the hunchback *was* of this type" (p. 20). And after the ballad maker tells the story of the miserable lives of the Macy children, the lamenting voice explains what this background does to Henry Macy:

> But the hearts of small children *are* delicate organs. A cruel beginning in this world *can twist* them into curious shapes. The heart of a hurt child *can shrink* so that forever afterward it is hard and pitted as the seed of a peach. Or again, the heart of such a child *may fester* and *swell* until it is a misery to carry within the body, easily chafed and hurt by the most ordinary things. This last is what happened to Henry Macy, who is so opposite to his brother, is the kindest and gentlest man in town. (p. 29)

Of the two voices of the narrator, the one which tells the love story, the actual narrative, is the dominant one. This voice is the objective voice of the literary ballad maker. On this level, McCullers chooses past tense verb forms, simple diction, a large percentage of simple sentences, often as short as three or four words, compound sentences with short members, and realistic dialog. The dialog is in rural Georgia dialect and comprises a very small percentage of the total narrative, actually less than one hundred and fifty lines. Like Eudora Welty, McCullers relies entirely on syntax and local idiom to convey the speech patterns of these rural milltown people. She does not employ distortion of spelling to convey variances in pronunciation. Although the narrator implies that long hours of the long, hot summers and dreary winters were spent in telling tall tales, little actual evidence of any prolonged conversation exists in the novel. Only once is there a sustained conversation between Miss Amelia and Cousin Lymon:

> "Amelia, what does it signify?" Cousin Lymon asked her.
> "Why, it's just an acorn," she answered. "Just an acorn I picked up on the afternoon Big Papa died."
> "How do you mean?" Cousin Lymon insisted.
> "I mean it's just an acorn I spied on the ground that day. I picked it up and put it in my pocket. But I don't know why."
> "What a peculiar reason to keep it," Cousin Lymon said. (p. 36)

In an apparent imitation of the poetic ballad, McCullers constructs paragraphs which are rather uniform in length, about one hundred and fifty words each. Many of these paragraphs begin with very short simple sentences in subject–verb order:

> The place was not always a cage. (p. 4)
> Dark came on. (p. 15)
> And Miss Amelia married him. (p. 30)
> They were wrong. (p. 31)
> The hunchback chattered on. (p. 40)
> Henry Macy was still silent. (p. 42)
> The hunchback was impatient. (p. 43)
> The autumn was a happy time. (p. 44)
> No one answered. (p. 49)
> Miss Amelia made no protest. (p. 59)
> The snow did not last. (p. 60)
> So things went on like this. (p. 62)
> The rest is confusion. (p. 68)

Additionally in the literary ballad form McCullers employs alliteration, repetition, and poetic imagery. Running throughout the narrative are repeated references to Miss Amelia's "ten-day marriage," "the loom-fixer," "the August white heat," "the peach trees," "the golden dust." She paints her background canvas with color imagery:

> The *red* winter sun was setting, and to the west the sky was deep *gold* and *crimson*. (p. 48)

The next morning was serene, with a sunrise of warm *purple* mixed with rose. In the fields around the town the furrows were newly plowed, and very early the tenants were at work setting out the young, deep *green* tobacco plants. The wild crows flew down close to the fields, making *swift blue* shadows on the earth. In the town the people set out early with their dinner pails, and the windows of the mill were blinding *gold* in the sun. (p. 12)

McCullers most frequently employs alliteration and sensory images, often combining the two:

The moon made dim, twisted shadows of the blossoming peach trees along the side of the road. In the air the odor of blossoms and *s*weet *s*pring grass mingled with the warm, *s*our *s*mell of the nearby lagoon. (p. 6)

The night was silent and the moon *s*till *s*hone with a *s*oft, clear light—it was getting colder. (p. 9)

The lamp on the table was well-trimmed, *b*urning *b*lue at the edges of the wick and casting a cheerful light in the kitchen. (p. 12)

The two voices of the single narrator alternate and together weave the tale of the lover, the beloved and of love betrayed. The ballad voice tells the story, and the second voice provides the sad background music. The styles of the two voices are distinctly different in syntax also. In the ballad teller's voice, McCullers rarely employs complex sentences. When they are used, they are almost always in normal order with single right-branching clauses. The most common of these structures is the noun modifier rather than an adverbial modifier. Unlike the simple sentences which often have tricolon verb structures with the last member expanded, the complex sentences usually employ either a single verb or a compound verb. On the other hand, the lamenting voice is related in complex sentences in periodic order with multiple clauses that are both adverbial and adjectival. These structures often employ self-embeddings along with multiple nominals and verbals.

This analysis would seem to imply that one voice is entirely separate from the other; that, however, is not the case. The transitions from one voice to the other are smooth, almost unnoticeable. One of the transitional devices that McCullers employs to move from one to the other is the question and answer. The ballad teller asks a question, and the lamenting voice answers it:

What sort of thing, then was this love?

First of all, love is a joint experience between two persons—but the fact that it is a joint experience to the two people involved. There are the lover and the beloved, but these two come from different countries. Often the beloved is only a stimulus for all the stored-up love which has lain quiet within the lover for a long time hitherto. And somehow every lover knows this. He feels in his soul that his love is a solitary thing. He comes to know a new, strange loneliness and it is this knowledge which makes him suffer. So there is only one thing for the lover to do. He must house his lover within himself as best he can; he must create for himself a whole new inward world—a world intense and strange, complete in himself. (p. 26)

The most frequently used device is the shift from the particular action of the mill-town group to the lamenting voice's generalization about that pattern of behavior among all people, as when McCullers moves from a description of Henry Macy as a child to her generalization about all such miserable children, or from Miss Amelia's liquor to the effects of liquor in general. This particular technique also permits transition again to the narrative in the reverse pattern of general to particular. For example, after the ballad teller has described the birth of the café, the lamenting voice comments on the general behavior of people in cafés, and the ballad teller follows this philosophical comment with the behavior of Miss Amelia's customers:

But the spirit of a café is altogether different. Even the richest, greediest old rascal will behave himself, insulting no one in a proper café. And poor people look about them gratefully and pinch up the salt in a dainty and modest manner. For the atmosphere of a proper café implies these qualities: fellowship, the satisfactions of the belly, and a certain gaiety and grace of behavior. This had never been told to the gathering in Miss Amelia's store that night. But they knew it of themselves, although never, of course, until that time had there been a café in the town. (p. 23)

The third method of transition from one voice to the other employed by McCullers is the time shift from the past of the story to the present. Of course the novel begins and ends in the present in the "dreary" mill town, but constantly within the frame of this time, the reader is swept back from the lively past into the present. The reader is carefully reminded that "it all happened long ago" (p. 27).

After the narrator's two voices are silent, after the sad story has been told, McCullers attaches the epilogue "Twelve Mortal Men." Barbara Nauer Folk believes that this epilogue serves to remind the reader that the story is both a "literary ballad and a folk dirge." What Folk is isolating in form as "dual-level usage of the ballad form"[6] is stylistically the dual voices of the single narrator. The harmony of the voices of the "twelve mortal men, seven of them black and five of them white boys from this county" (p. 72) is precisely the kind of harmony McCullers achieves in the blending of the two voices of her single narrator. For the objective voice that relates the sequence of events of the narrative, McCullers chooses short, almost choppy sentences in normal order and casts the verbs in the past tense. For the subjective, lamenting voice, she employs long sentences with multiple embeddings, present tense verb forms, and frequent imperatives that order the reader to interpret the bare details given by the other voice. These two voices serve McCullers in the same way that various instruments within an orchestra serve the conductor. The harmony is not achieved because the various musicians are reacting to the same notes; it relies upon the instructions of that conductor. That the two distinctly different narrative voices in *The Ballad of the Sad Café* are not in discord is a tribute to the author's ability to convey these voices in two recognizably different yet compatible rhetorical styles.

NOTES

1. Lawrence Graver, *Carson McCullers* (Minneapolis: University of Minnesota Press, 1969), p. 24.

2. Dayton Kohler, "Carson McCullers: Variations on a Theme," *College English*, 13 (1951), 8.

3. Dawson P. Gaillard, "The Presence of the Narrator in Carson McCullers' *The Ballad of the Sad Café*," *Mississippi Quarterly* 25 (1972), 419.

4. Joseph R. Millichap, "Carson McCullers' Literary Ballad," *Georgia Review*, 27 (1973), 330.

5. Carson McCullers, *The Ballad of the Sad Café and Other Stories* (1951; rpt. New York: Bantam, 1969) p. 3. All subsequent quotations are from this edition of the novel.

6. Barbara Nauer Folk, "The Sad Sweet Music of Carson McCullers," *Georgia Review*, 16 (1962), 203.

RUTH M. VANDE KIEFT

The Love Ethos of Porter, Welty, and McCullers

Since love is a central theme in much fiction, especially that of women writers, it is not surprising to find the theme dominant in the fiction of Katherine Anne Porter, Eudora Welty, and Carson McCullers. What is surprising, given their time and place in the most conservative part of the country, the South (Texas, Mississippi, Georgia) in the first half of the twentieth century, is the extent to which each writer, though she could not totally escape conventional codes and attitudes toward love, essentially subverted them in her life as a fiction writer. Their contrasting lives and fictional projections of love reveal how as artists they individually fulfilled their destinies and escaped from the common female destiny, the stories society might have written for them, and they for their characters, as lovers, wives, and mothers.

In my essay, I analyze and relate these two sets of stories, the biographical and fictional "love lives" of the three writers. I am aware of the hazards of my undertaking: chiefly its magnitude and the impossibility of sorting out facts from fiction. For in what other area of a woman's life is reality more infused with fantasy, is language more "loaded" and ungovernable, are assumptions, actions, values more charged and elusive in their meanings?

I face these difficulties squarely and attempt to deal with them in two

From *The Female Tradition in Southern Literature*, edited by Carol S. Manning. © 1993 by the Board of Trustees of the University of Illinois.

ways. First, I use the term *mythos* because it implies a pattern of attitudes and experiences that are both individual and yet shared with others in smaller or larger groups. For each of the three writers, there is, in addition to a unique personal history, a set of "conventional" (religious, archetypal, literary) sources of the mythos that the writer either wholly or partially accepts or rejects. Each has her own relationship to "the truth," each a different way of conducting her life and using it in her fiction, a different mix of the realistic with the fantastic. Each writer's "mythos of love" is the intricately woven pattern of several components: (1) her early experiences within the family setting; (2) her "love history" as a woman; and (3) her imaginative assimilation of both traditional and modern attitudes toward love acquired through formal education, reading, observation. Each component is to some extent cloaked in its own language and reference system, the community's encoding of attitudes and assumptions. Since I cannot treat all elements consistently or at equal length, I shall stress what seem the most important formative influences on each writer.

Second, I have limited my study to the fiction itself and material essentially biographical rather than critical. Fortunately, for two of the writers we have long, definitive, authorized biographies written by sympathetic women: Joan Givner's of Porter and Virginia Spencer Carr's of McCullers. In Welty's case, we have a slender autobiography, *One Writer's Beginnings*, itself a work of art, though not, I think, another of her works of fiction, for I believe it to be as honest as it is beautiful, moving, and amusing, however selective in its personal revelations. These biographical sources being different from each other in kind and approach, I make no claims for their comparative objectivity, or that of my own conclusions. Since the territory I hope to survey is thickly wooded, I intend to be wary, flexible, and suggestive rather than definitive or doctrinaire.

1

Porter's mythos of love seems the most perilous of the three to describe because, though convoluted, it is easiest to reduce to a formula: the Freudian one of the wholly determining effects of early childhood on all of a writer's work. In an extraordinary feat of fact-gathering and reconstruction, Givner has told Porter's life story and revealed her life-long habit of interweaving fact, fantasy, and fiction. Porter invented for herself a Southern aristocratic past and early family history. She assumed and played out the dual roles of Southern belle modernized and liberated, and legendary femme fatale. Her beauty, love of finery in clothing and decor and exoticism in food and drink, her four marriages and countless love affairs, her self-infatuated conversations, her restless traveling and adventures, her uncanny timing in being in the right place at the right time to involve herself with important historical persons and events—all this is the stuff of a legend she self-consciously created, a legend more usually associated with Hollywood stars than one devoted to a craft that invites what Welty once referred to as "the intimacy of strangers."

Givner's "uneasy sense," expressed in the prologue to her biography, "that the revelations about [Porter's] life constituted some cruel kind of exposure" (22), seems justified, for it is an often vain, selfish, capricious, exploitive, irresponsible, deceitful character that emerges. Yet Givner salvages respect and admiration for Porter, whose actual life she found "more heroic than anything [Porter] invented" (23), for it is the story of a sensitive child named Callie whose mother died when she was two years old; who was raised in miserable poverty and overcrowding in a large household by a strict Methodist grandmother; who was neglected, erratically treated and unloved by a weak and self-indulgent father; whose amorous adventures were the compulsive attempts of a love-starved woman to find what she could not possibly attain. Givner's commissioned biography seems the fruit of Porter's decision to "come clean," make a truthful final confession, not only to a priest but to the world. Yet whatever her relation to the truth, in her personal legend making, Porter was exhibiting a characteristically Southern trait.

The encoded rhetoric that lies behind Porter's ethos of love has both a popular and a traditional source, each of which I think she had unconsciously assimilated, insofar as the rhetoric fed some impossible idealism about romantic love that she seems never to have lost. The popular source is best illustrated by excerpts from letters Porter's father, Harrison, wrote shortly after the death of his wife, Alice, samples of the kind of sentimental graveyard rhetoric satirized by Mark Twain in *Huckleberry Finn*. The first letter, to his oldest daughter, was sent with a picture:

> Gay: This is your mother. She is buried near Brownwood. It is a holy place for us all. There I saw the star of all my earthly hopes go down in an endless darkness and there is no light in my heart even at noonday. In this strange twilight I try to trace the narrow road I must walk to reach this city of the dead and lie down in the long night beside my love. But this star is not extinguished altogether for it shed the rays of its purity and love over the waste landscape of my life, gave meaning to Nothingness and left memories that not time nor death itself can take away. (Givner 40)

To a close friend of Alice he wrote: "I loved her better than my own life, aye, better than I did my God.... If there is, after this turmoil, a halcyon period, a golden place somewhere 'en vista' of the golden dawn, I know my spirit will seek hers there, though but a season. Hell thenceforth with the companionship of the Dragon of the Apocalypse will not torment me worse than the pangs that now rend me" (Givner 40–41).

From this graveyard rhetoric it is a short leap to that of the poem Uncle Gabriel writes to memorialize his beloved Amy in "Old Mortality ("A singing angel, she forgets / The griefs of old mortality" [Porter, *Stories* 181]). Noteworthy about Harrison Porter's rhetoric, in addition is its self-indulgence, is its "literary" pretension and the mixing of religious language with that of human love. Harrison plays out his drama as mourner on a cosmic stage against a backdrop of time and eternity, heaven and hell, salvation and damnation. And Porter played out her drama on the same cosmic stage.

The other encoded rhetoric is that of the ancient noble literary tradition of Courtly Love, the Age of Chivalry. The love ethos is often adulterous, thriving most when unconsummated, product of fevered imaginations, high codes of morality and tests of bravery, celebrated by poets of stature from the Middle Ages to the nineteenth-century Romantics. Actually, this noble tradition reached the South, and doubtless Porter, more by way of Sir Walter Scott than Dante, Shakespeare, and Keats. Porter had little formal education and was not an inveterate reader as a child. Her fictional portrayal of what had become of the Western world's and the South's version of love is negative: she shows love traduced and betrayed, relentlessly exposed and rejected, yet also as inescapable and hopelessly victimizing. The romantic and antiromantic are constantly at war in Porter's fiction; her pages are strewn with the combatants wounded, dying, and dead of that mortal struggle.

It is instructive to look closely at the battle in its formative stages, to Miranda's, that is, Porter's generation as it appears in "Old Mortality." Miranda and her sister Maria, eight and twelve years old, are deeply impressed by the story of Aunt Amy, who, though now only a "ghost in a frame," had once been "beautiful, much loved, unhappy, and had died young." Though somewhat skeptical about the romantic legends told by their elders, the little girls enjoy "patching together ... fragments of tales that were like bits of poetry, and music ... with the theatre." The romance of their Uncle Gabriel's "long, unrewarded love for [Amy], her early death," was a story linked for them with books they thought of as "unworldly ... but true, such as the Vita Nuova, the Sonnets of Shakespeare and the Wedding Song of Spenser; and poems by Edgar Allan Poe" (178). Thus an ancient and noble lineage of love poetry is provided for Porter's fictional counterpart, Miranda, though there is little to indicate that these greatest of love poets were early a seriously formative part of Porter's actual reading and thinking. Yet as central to her fictive world, they provided her with the norm for the lofty and unattainable ("unworldly") ideal of love she saw everywhere traduced.

Amy is presented as willful, capricious, a type of La Belle Dame Sans Merci. She dresses and behaves scandalously, has many beaus while resisting the courtship of Miranda's profligate Uncle Gabriel, has a duel fought over her and compensates for life's dullness by running off, half-sick, on a three-day lark to the border with her brothers. She perversely accepts Gabriel when he loses his family inheritance, marries him in a gray wedding gown, and dies within ten days, not only of chronic illness, but, it is hinted, an overdose of medication. Miranda is impressed by this history, and although she already knows how far reality is from the romantic legends enshrined in the family memory, she persists in her addiction to the romantic gesture, as in her rebellion against conventional morality. Her alternately strict and indulgent rearing makes satirical comedy of the emphasis on character training taught by the nuns in the convent school in which Miranda and her sister are "inured." Their father reinforces the superficiality of the Catholic moral codes by stressing his daughters' need to be good chiefly in order to win the reward of being swept off to the races on certain "blessed Saturdays."

Miranda elopes from out of the convent at sixteen and flees from the marriage within two years. Desperately in love, Porter herself married at sixteen in a double wedding with her sister, a civil ceremony conducted by a Methodist minister. Though the marriage lasted nine years, the longest of her marriages, the relationship was a disaster. Porter later referred to her husband, John Koontz, as a "monster"—a term she applied to all her husbands and lovers. Givner speculates that Porter's inability to find any pleasure in sex ... aggravated furthermore by her discovery that she was not able to bear a child" (92) was the cause for her romantic disillusionment. In the final section of "Old Mortality" Porter has Miranda think, after her divorce, "I hate loving and being loved. I hate it," and then suffer "a shock of comfort from the sudden collapse of an old painful structure of distorted images and misconceptions" (221).

Yet Miranda rejects also her ugly, chinless, peppermint-breathed feminist cousin Eva in Eva's reductive assessment of Amy's romantic history as "just sex!" What else but desire for romantic love—with its rich fantasy, brief and ambiguous pleasure, and almost inevitable disillusionment and pain—could have induced Porter's fictional characters to act as they did? "Old Mortality" ends with Miranda's thinking, "I don't want any promises, I won't have false hopes, I won't be romantic about myself.... At least I can know the truth about what happens to me, she assured herself silently, making a promise to herself, in her hopelessness, her ignorance" (221). The final word shows how little Porter believed that Miranda, or anyone, could find the truth for herself, unshackle herself from the past or even settle for the bleak reductions of the present. Porter found her truth only in the realm of what she created, the means and end of her integrity and her personal salvation, her fictional art. And in her choice of the free, bohemian existence and refusal of the traditional roles of strong, supportive wife and mother, she became a prototype of the modern woman artist.

The Miranda stories tell a bitter story about love—with one exception, "Pale Horse, Pale Rider." But that story presents romantic love as mythical, Edenic. Miranda's soldier-lover is named Adam—obviously prelapsarian; he is described as being round, firm, and beautiful as an unbitten apple; he is even compared to the sacrificial lamb. The pale horse and rider of the Apocalypse, death, carries him off sinless, and before his and Miranda's love is consummated. There is no grand passion: only the sweet elusiveness of an ideal lost love. The encoded language is religious—hymns, prayers, the Bible—from Genesis to Revelation, Eden to the fourth horseman of the Apocalypse (death) to a viewed and missed Paradise beyond; the love language is innocent—that of simple Western ballads.

The finality of death is the seal on a perfect love that might be viewed as Porter's imaginative reenactment of the love of her mother and father. In later life Porter idealized the young man on whom she modeled Adam—apparently a young English soldier who lived in the same rooming house, looked after her before a hospital bed could be found, kissed her once, and died of influenza while she was ill. She made of this casual acquaintance the man she might have trusted and been happy with all her days. "This lifelong devotion," says Givner, "should properly be seen as the love of a writer for a favorite character, the love of an artist for the created object. There is, therefore, an ironic truth in her assertion that he was the one man she could have loved" (129).

Miranda, the survivor, denied her bright vision of death, is seen in the end as a silver-gray ghost, though a very smartly dressed one, with her beautiful smooth gray gloves. Salvation through style: that too was Porter's modus vivendi as she took up her life after her rub with death. In stories based more purely on her own experience, Porter achieves a group of painfully authentic, psychologically acute portraits of the failures of modern love. Givner describes how the patterns of confusion, tension, and dissolution developed from a "fatal ambivalence" in Porter's nature. She craved an adoring, protective kind of masculine love she never got from her weak father, or for a great length of time from any of her husbands and lovers, since it would have been one requiring a docile and obedient wife or mistress to complete on the receiving side. Yet she also had the desire to be a strong, dominant and independent woman like her grandmother. Her apparent distaste for the sexual relationship and her apparent inability to bear children further threatened her fragile sense of her femininity and desirability (Givner 89–93).

In story after story, Porter presents stormy quarrels between lovers and the unconvincing calms or reconciliations that follow them; she shows destructive fury striking out blindly. To the heroine of "Theft," survivor of many painful love affairs, the loss of a beautiful, golden cloth purse reflects "the long patient suffering of dying friendships and the dark, inexplicable death of love" in a landslide of remembered losses" (*Stories* 64). In the end she thinks, "I was right not to be afraid of any thief but myself, who will end by leaving me nothing" (65). In these stories love is elusive and illusionary yet eternally revived as though in answer to some demon of obsession.

This misanthropy and cynicism about love reaches a series of frenzied peaks in *Ship of Fools*. The feeling between David darling and Jenny angel passes quickly and irrationally from loving passion to fierce hatred, the flux of emotion touched off by the slightest impression, such as the couple's reactions to Jenny's appearance in a fresh white dress. When David sees her as lovely, and tells her so, the narrator says, "She believed it with all her heart, and saw him transfigured as he always was in these mysterious visitations of love between them—reasonless, causeless, having its own times and seasons, vanishing at a breath and yet always bringing with it the illusion that it would last forever" (*Ship of Fools* 422). Yet, after seeing Jenny drunk in another man's embrace, David comes to think that "the girl he thought he knew had disappeared so entirely he had almost to believe he made her up out of the odds and ends of stuff from his own ragbag of adolescent dreams and imaginings.... There never was, there couldn't possibly be, any such living girl as he had dreamed Jenny was" (450).

Dr. Schumann, the ship's physician, loves La Condessa but does not comfort her by giving any sign of his love until very shortly before she leaves the ship in political custody. The irony is that he is illicitly feeding the Condessa's drug addiction and thus killing her. A Mrs. Treadwell, divorced and bitter, remembers her "despairs, her long weeping, her miserable grief over the failure of love" (481). She unleashes such mindless fury against aggressive male sexuality that she makes pulp of the face of a young man with the sharp pointed heel of her evening slipper when he comes to the cabin in lustful pursuit of her young cabin-mate. All three of the "heroines" of *Ship of Fools*, as Givner points out, are avatars of Porter at some state of her life in a typical love relationship.

Whereas this psychologically acute fiction is painful, often self-lacerating in its personal revelation, in other stories Porter makes the imaginative leap into persons unlike herself, relating their experiences with empathy and compassion as well as fidelity to the particulars of their time and place. In "Flowering Judas" she shows the plight of a modern young woman who has lost the Catholic faith of her childhood and can replace it neither with the Socialist faith of the Mexican Revolution nor the personal faith and purpose of romantic or maternal love. In "Noon Wine" she portrays a weak poverty-stricken woman, Mrs. Thompson, testifying against her conscience, in support of her morally weak husband. She is defeated by fate and social codes in a society as dominated by male supremacy as is Sicily or Mexico.

In other of Porter's stories, however, women are far from weak and defeated in relation to their men. Maria Concepcion accomplishes her own revenge on her sexual rival by killing her and taking the girl's child as her own. "Granny Weatherall" nourishes a life-long grievance against the man who jilted her and risks hell rather than surrender that hatred, even on her deathbed. These women are strong enough to take risks that may cost them their lives, for time and eternity. In their fight against male hegemony, they might appear to be champions of female independence until one looks closely at what each of these women desires. It is the love of her man, the fulfillment of the promise or vow he made and broke; it is position in the community, marriage, the child by him she expects. These are women who embrace traditional feminine roles with a vengeance. Porter knows much of woman's consciousness and dilemmas in love but nothing of their cure, and she does not fictionalize her own personal "cure" of self-realization through her art.

What fascinates in Porter's personal and fictional love experiences, finally, is the tension between extreme idealism and scepticism, traditional romance and realistic modern attitudes. A clear-eyed appraisal of herself told her how foolish and brief were her many affairs, how much based on fictions spun out of the imagination. And yet she had a feeling that there was also, in the love object, an actual love and beauty that answered her need and capacity for discovering and offering her own; and that, when this idealization was mutual in a relationship, it was wonderfully transforming. When she fell in love, her partner was "instantly transfigured with a light of such blinding brilliance all natural attributes disappear[ed]" and an "archangel" appeared, "beautiful, flawless in temperament, witty, intelligent, charming, of ... infinite grace, sympathy, and courage." This is the golden god of romantic love. It was inevitable that such great expectations should again and again suffer disillusionment. She called it "'probably the silliest kind of love there is, but I am glad I had it. I'm glad there were times when I saw human beings at their best, for I don't think by any means I lent them all their radiance'" (Givner 336).

Porter was a fierce and often intolerant woman, requiring impeccable manners but failing in trust and fidelity. Legendary in all things, she was above all that in her primary dedication to her art. Admired and hated with equal fervor, she has been accused of many character flaws but never of being a less than committed and formidably gifted fiction writer.

2

That Porter should have approved of Eudora Welty and her fiction is not surprising. This shy and gentle woman with her obvious artistic talent evoked Porter's praise. Porter was an early supporter of Welty's work, which she encouraged by writing an introduction to Welty's first collection of stories, *A Curtain of Green*. Many years later Welty repaid that debt with her discerning lecture on Porter's work, which she made the title essay of her collection of nonfictional writing, *The Eye of the Story*. In it, she comments on Porter's antiromantic vision of love, stating, "All the stories she has written are moral stories about love and the hate that is love's twin, love's imposter and enemy and death. Rejection, betrayal, theft roam the pages of her stories as they roam the world.... All this is a way of showing to the inward eye: Look at what you are doing to love" (*Eye* 33–34).

Welty's comments about Porter's stories are indicative of the contrasts between the two writers' ethos of love and the experiences that lay behind them. Instead of the poverty-stricken, love-starved, motherless Callie, we find, in Welty's account of her childhood in *One Writer's Beginnings*, a child secure in the love and protection of parents who loved each other deeply and her with the special care and concern of a couple who had lost their first born and themselves had lost parents at an early age. She describes her habit of half-listening in on her parents' intimate conversations after she had been put to bed, feeling herself "present in the room with the chief secret there was—the two of them, father and mother, there as one." This made her feel included, exercising when young "the turn of mind, the nature of temperament, of a privileged observer ... [of] the loving kind" (21). One might say that her parents and their love are the muses of Welty's art: she seems almost to invoke them in her epigraph to her autobiography, which she also dedicates to them. Such parental influence is beneficent, except for the necessary loss of independence anyone much loved experiences, especially when that love is strongly reciprocal, when the child is shy, and (though she does not say so) the protection is especially strong because it is of a girl in that Southern place and time. She experienced a feeling of guilt as she gradually broke away from her family's sheltering, though without ceasing to love them deeply.

The necessary independence was accomplished by her being away at college, then for a year in New York City (where she studied advertising at Columbia University); traveling around the state of Mississippi doing publicity work for the Works Projects Administration; continuing to make frequent trips to New York trying to sell her photographs and stories. But already as a child she had begun to achieve her inner freedom and sense of adventure through her wide reading and active imagination, her fascination with stories of all kinds—fairy tales, myths, children's fiction, family stories, and local histories and legends, which were as indigenous to her southern region as the landscape. At Wisconsin, as an English major, she studied literature and came to know many of the great "canonical" writers, including the moderns, such as Yeats and Chekhov. All this made for breadth in Eudora Welty's love ethos, as ancient fictions were assimilated to the lives and experiences of people she saw and knew. She tapped the mythical and archetypal—their symbols and personifications—a dimension always evident in her work, sometimes boldly, as in *The Robber Bridegroom*, sometimes more subtly, as in *The Golden Apples*.

Classically "romantic" attitudes about love are seen in an autobiographical story in which the narrator tells about her own experience of first love, "A Memory." Here, she describes the two worlds in which she lived as a child: as observer, making frames with her hands to look out at and identify everything, imposing order on confusion; as dreamer, in her feelings for a small blond classmate. "I was in love then for the first time: I had identified love at once" (*Stories*, 76). The love, brought into being by an accidental touching of wrists on the stair, exists entirely in her dream world, since the two children are not even friends and the boy knows nothing about the passion he has innocently evoked. Significantly, the love is *protective*—the girl is fearful about the dangers that might befall her beloved; she faints when he has a sudden nosebleed in class: only thus does the imagined and threatening "real world" of the boy darken her dream of love. And that dream, in turn, is crashed into by an "unwelcome realism" of a group of fat, ugly, vulgar bathers in the violence they perpetrate on their own and each others' bodies and the beach. Of the dreamer's love, Welty says in *One Writer's Beginnings*, "Amorphous and tender, from now on it will have to remain hidden, her own secret imagining" (89).

The two images—of the frame (rigid, removed, objective yet coercive in her hands, imposing order where life always threatens chaos) and the dream (amorphous, boundless, vagrant)—are equivalents of the polarity evident in Welty's love ethos at its two extremes: at once highly romantic yet realistic. That we have no knowledge of Welty's later personal experience of love beyond that first love described as "hopelessly unexpressed within me and grotesquely altered in the outward world" (*Stories*, 76)—subjective, internal, unrealistic—means no more than that Welty has always been reticent about the private life that lay behind the shy but gracious manner of a writer who remained single, practiced her craft and stayed mostly at home (much of the time with a widowed mother), made frequent trips to New York, traveled often to Europe and around the United States, and became a publicly honored and widely loved American fiction writer. A single remark dropped incidentally in *One Writer's Beginnings*, by way of her differentiating her actual self from the fictional character she feels closest to because of their shared passion for their art (Miss Eckhart of *The Golden Apples*), about having not "miss[ed] out in love" (101), suggests what no one might have reason to doubt from her fiction: firsthand experience of love. But she does not use that experience directly, as Porter did. Nor could she write about people to whom she was close—"those known to you in ways too deep, too overflowing, ever to be plumbed outside love." Instead, she states, "what I do make stories out of is the whole fund of my feelings, my responses to the real experiences of my own life, to the relationships that formed and changed it, that I have given most of myself to, and so learned my way toward a dramatic counterpart" (100).

Considering Welty's love ethos as it emerges in her fiction after Porter's is like bursting out of heavy storms into sunshine. The comic intrudes almost everywhere in her fiction (even in so tragic a work as *The Optimist's Daughter*), providing balance, lending perspective. In Welty's fiction we have a complete and completed world of love: complete in that the full spectrum of kinds of love, both perennial and modern, is presented; completed in that characters are not usually left both betrayed and betraying, as they are in Porter's fiction, or (as we shall see) loose and unfinished, as in Carson McCullers's fiction. The theme being central to Welty's fiction, and her approaches to it so varied, some radical selection is necessary.

Welty's characters are often in some sort of predicament when it comes to love. They may be dimly aware of the need for fulfillment in love but are denied access to it. Clytie is thwarted by the members of her decaying aristocratic family, and Livvie by being married to her dignified old husband Solomon, whom she tends like a baby through his terminal illness. While Clytie concludes her search for the elusive face like her own by drowning herself in a rain barrel, Livvie is released and fulfilled when Solomon surrenders his life and Livvie to Cash, Solomon's field hand, young and beautiful to her. Livvie, ripe for sexual passion, requires no initiation. For

young Jenny in "At the Landing," it proves a harrowing experience as her
tenderly evolving virginal love endures the rough seizure of Billy Floyd, and
finally, multiple rape by violent river men.

Yet an almost worse predicament is one in which a male character is
ignorant of his overwhelming need for "A marriage, a fruitful marriage. That
simple thing. Anyone could have had that" (*Stories* 129). This is the tragic
realization of traveling salesman Bowman when he encounters such love in
the primitive, back-country Sonny and his pregnant wife ("Death of a
Traveling Salesman"). Exclusion seems to kill Bowman as much as does his
failing heart. Tom Harris, the traveling salesman of "The Hitch-Hikers,"
seems compelled to maintain his freedom from personal ties and
commitments; his unattached love contents itself with pity and small acts of
compassion such as he performs for the two tramps with whom he becomes
involved. Harris is wary of domination, which leads him to automatic
gestures of rejection, directed even at the nonthreatening and sweet young
Carol. By refusing a relationship with her, he is helplessly resigning himself
to his empty, rootless life on the road, a hitch-hiker who catches rides on
other people's experiences. Yet there is no bitterness in Welty's two
salesmen—mostly perplexity and weariness, the wistful sadness that comes
from hope constantly denied or quelled.

Welty's fiction often explores the conflicting claims of the self and the
other, even when love is fulfilled in marriage. Her lovers and mates are
shown as fighting attrition and overfamiliarity in love, refusing to make a
dreary set of habits of what began as excited discovery. Her women in
particular are independent, asking to be seen as always changing, not taken
for granted, inviolable in their center of self. In "The Wide Net," Hazel
causes her husband William Wallace to respect the mystery of her changing
body in pregnancy, the secret of her coming motherhood and his fatherhood;
and Ruby Fisher, in "A Piece of News," wants her dullard husband Clyde to
see her in the alien fantasy role she toys with in her casual adultery, as the
victim of his passionate jealousy—"beautiful, desirable, and dead" (*Stories*
14). If individual mystery must be protected, so must joy: in "The Bride of
the Innisfallen" this is called "primal joy," "the kind you were born and began
with" (*Stories* 517). In "Bride" a young American wife runs away from her
husband in London's grayness to Ireland's Cork in all its springtime glory, to
rediscover the exhilaration of private selfhood, of people and places, fresh as
dawn. For "love with the joy being drawn out of it," she feels, has "nearly
destroyed" her (*Stories* 517). These women will not be "killed" in their spirits
by the dullness or dominance of their mates. They subvert the conventional
codes of male supremacy as well as common wisdom about threats to the
marital state.

Welty's characters tend to be hopeful and resilient, for example, Virgie Rainey at the end of *The Golden Apples*. A woman in her early forties, she once supposed, like so many other young girls, that personal fulfillment lay in sexual pleasure, and so made love on a bare mattress with her sailor boyfriend in an abandoned house, then ran away with him to Memphis, and in so doing rejected her old piano teacher Miss Eckhart along with her Beethoven—and a special gift, the potential to become a great pianist. But Virgie had come back and had felt herself "undestroyed" walking across the golden fields toward her home town and her widowed mother. After her mother's death and many years of self-discipline, Virgie is now freed to begin a life of her own. In *One Writer's Beginnings* Welty says of Virgie: "Passionate, recalcitrant, stubbornly undefeated by failure or hurt or disgrace or bereavement, all the while heedlessly wasting of her gifts, she knows to the last that there is a world that remains out there, a world living and mysterious, and that she is of it" (102).

It is in her novels that Welty most fully explores the theme of love. *Delta Wedding* presents a large "extended" family with strong loyalties and traditions in a variety of love predicaments. Among these characters are two through whom Welty creates an ideal of love in action, Ellen and George Fairchild. They are not, however, a married couple but brother and sister-in-law. Ellen has married the oldest son in the Fairchild family, Battle, and does the mothering not only of her own large brood but of anyone who needs it, not through domineering nor coddling but through a deep understanding of individuals, seeking always in quiet, tactful ways to help those about her toward responsible maturity and personal fulfillment. She wisely shows how most conflict, including marital, lies within ourselves, not *between* us, and is "not over people" but "things like the truth, and what you owe people" (*Delta Wedding* 163). Her own center of self, appearing so fragile and feminine, is tough and durable, resembling the delicate, spiritually poised woman in Frost's "The Silken Tent" or Mrs. Ramsay in *To the Lighthouse*; most of all perhaps the famous portrait of *agape* in I Corinthians 13. All this is without benefit of a visible religious faith, though rising clearly from a Christian morality and reflecting, one might guess, the morality of Welty's own parents.

If Ellen Fairchild seems that not impossible she, George Fairchild does seem that impossible he. Welty tried to make him as credibly human and faulty as she made him heroic, ideal, charismatic, but it was a perilous undertaking. That is, as I see it, because she tried to graft a type of *agape* onto human love outside the framework of the Christian faith. George is made to be and act much like Christ—or at least the St. George who slew the dragon—while often resembling neither, but rather Dionysus, Pang or King

McLain of *The Golden Apples*. He also appears to have the psychological complexity and sophistication of a modern man.

The initiating action of the novel is George's saving an idiot niece from an oncoming train, the Yellow Dog. This heroic risk taking is related to what the love ethos of the novel presents as life's greatest risk, marriage; George has compounded that risk by "marrying down"—a pretty girl, Robbie, who worked in the plantation store. His double risk precipitates Dabney Fairchild's decision to marry Troy, the plantation overseer, a man twice her age with a mountain country background: she too is "marrying down." To Robbie, George's heroism on the train track reveals what she regards as his thralldom to the Fairchilds, his greater concern for the idiot daughter of dear dead Dennis, the family hero, than for her and their possible (unborn) child.

But sensitive members of the family know that not only devotion to the Fairchilds and their traditions motivates George's love. Dabney perceives that though "the very heart of the family," he is "different from them." His risk taking includes separating two little Negro boys fighting dangerously with knives, embracing them as well as family members. Dabney had protested against that—"all the Fairchild in her had screamed at his interfering ... caring about anything in the world but them." She is awed at the kind of sweetness that "could be the visible surface of profound depths— the surface of all the darkness that might frighten her.... George loved *the world*, something told her suddenly. Not them! Not them in particular" (*Delta Wedding* 36, 37). The language evoked here is clearly biblical: "For God so loved the world." George's love is as universal as divine love in its confrontation of all that is dark and terrifying in human life, in its selfless sacrifice and detachment, though with its capacity also for special attachments. Its end product is an active, courageous participation in all human life, a life of suffering sustained, terrors met and subdued. George the beloved, the peace maker, is apart from the family that mothers him indulgently and yet relies upon him as its conscience and protector. He has the quality of waiting or withholding, curbing his strength while some frail or tentative life asks to be nurtured. The motherless child Laura sees this quality and responds with ardor. George's wife, Robbie, learns, with pain and humiliation, that his love can never be exclusive. George *must* love the whole world—not her exclusively.

One brief mysterious incident helps to fill out Welty's concept of the nature of George and his and Ellen's love. Though both are loyal spouses and harbor no secret adulterous passion for each other, their deep mutual understanding makes them sister souls. Ellen is searching in the woods for her lost garnet pin when she comes upon a half-wild lost girl who seems to "*shed beauty*," nymph-like, "a creature not hiding, but waiting to be seen"

(70). Ellen tries to warn this nymph of the danger of her unprotected position, but the girl wants to know the road toward Memphis, "the old Delta synonym for pleasure, trouble, and shame." Ellen says, "I'm not stopping you," and the girl says comfortably, "You couldn't stop me" (70–71). But someone apparently can.

Later, when Ellen tells George about meeting the girl, he says, "Yes, I took her over to the old Argyle gin and slept with her." Ellen is shocked but withholds judgment, mulls over George's action and failure to excuse or explain what he has done, and finally concludes that he was "the one person she knew in the world who did not have it in him to make of any act a facile thing or to make a travesty out of human beings—even, in spite of temptation at a time like this moment, of *himself* as one human being.... Only George left the world she knew as pure—in spite of his fierce energies, even heresies—as he found it; still real, still bad, still fleeting and mysterious and hopelessly alluring to her" (79–80). Ellen sees that her fear for the whole family has been projected onto the girl. So George has absorbed not only the lost girl's sexual need but Ellen's anxiety about her own daughters' sexual rites of passage, with no excuses for his act. He has slain the dragon both for Ellen and the lost girl (whose desire for passion and adventure is fulfilled). But clearly, *heresy* is the right word for it, as for what Welty has done with that character in that act. And Welty disposes of the girl rather too conveniently by having her killed by the Yellow Dog. Since George seems too paradoxically idealized a character—half Christian, half pagan—to be quite credible, he might be thought of as Welty's fictional projection of a complex ideal of modern manhood—what Adam was to Porter. Much of George's generous and universal human love (*agape*) is also to be found in the young hero of *Losing Battles*, Jack Renfro, though he lacks George's intelligence and sophistication.

Welty's most mature vision of love is to be found in the last and most autobiographical of her novels, *The Optimist's Daughter*. The background of the wife and mother of the novel, Becky McKelva, is identical to that of Welty's own mother. In the McKelva family, Welty shows the same kind of ardent and protective love she herself had known at home, though with important differences: Laurel Hand, the McKelva's daughter, is an only child (Welty had two younger brothers); Laurel was briefly married to Philip Hand during World War II and soon widowed; and Judge McKelva, the father, is a Southerner, unlike Christian Welty (from Ohio, a Northerner like Philip). Welty shows the characters' protecting and protesting in their deep love and concern for each other, to the point where it becomes limiting of personal freedom, and finally, under the blight of illness (literal sight problems become symbolic of inner loss of vision), almost abusive. Judge

McKelva's protective love leads to a need to indulge women (a possible indictment on Welty's part of superficial Southern male gallantry). This turns into a form of self-indulgence as he marries his second wife, the cheap, self-centered Fay Chisom. The result, as Laurel perceives, is her father's suffering then from too little rather than too much love. And in the last years of her life Becky—blind, half-crazed from desperation, her reason crippled by strokes—feels abandoned by her husband and daughter. Laurel's tragic discovery is that love can remain perfect only when it has been frozen in time by the early death of the beloved (thus Laurel with Philip). Subject to the hazards of time, chance, sickness, death, no human love can remain perfect. Yet in memory it can be renewed, given continuity, even a form of permanence. This is the wise and weathered love of a survivor.

So far the vision of the child of "A Memory" has come. How very far from the vision of Porter in the work of her late maturity, *Ship of Fools*; for though Welty always combined a clear-eyed realism with deep romantic sympathies, and recognized how subjective and ephemeral love could be, her work is untouched by cynicism. For all the external restrictions of her life, in comparison with Porter's broad experience, she seems to have known and believed more about love and its potentials than did the legendary and glamorous Katherine Anne.

3

Though born only eight years after Eudora Welty in a Southern town (Columbia, Georgia) with codes and attitudes essentially like those of Welty's Jackson, in her love ethos Carson McCullers seems to have come from a totally different place and to have taken a giant step in time into the postmodern era of sexual liberation and tolerance of many kinds of sexual orientation. The paradox of McCullers is that she seems to combine the sophisticate with the ingenue or waif, as though she'd been born both old and innocent, achieved her full growth by adolescence (this she did literally, being so tall and lanky as a girl that she thought of herself as a freak), yet had never quite grown up. Like Porter and unlike Welty, she seems to have lived her life self-consciously, dramatically, intermingling the world of fiction or fantasy and reality.

Although Virginia Spencer Carr, in her biography of Carson McCullers, *The Lonely Hunter*, does stress what is unusual in the childhood of Lula Carson Smith, there is no immediate way to get from the facts to a small body of fiction that begins when she is in her late teens; opens with a pair of deaf mute homosexuals strolling arm in arm; and includes a man who drives a nail through his hand and fastens it to the table, a sexually frustrated woman who cuts off her nipples with a pair of garden clippers, and a love match between a powerful, mannish woman and a dwarf. There isn't even a way to anticipate McCullers's central theme, which Carr identifies as "loneliness, isolation, and estrangement," a condition in which "reciprocity in a love relationship seemed impossible" and in which "the norms were normlessness, meaninglessness, purposelessness, powerlessness, and alienation" (2). Surely she was loved but by a strong, ambitious, dominating mother who was convinced that her child was a genius and who showed tendencies to nonconformity and the flouting of convention. McCullers's father, a jeweler, seems to have been more conventional, and rather distant from his daughter. This lack of a solid paternal influence may have contributed to McCullers's sexual ambivalence, as her mother's dominance contributed to the ambivalence she always felt about her two paradoxical needs: to be separate, independent, uniquely gifted; and to belong, be dependent, a member merging her identity with that of others. What Porter seized for herself in the absence of parental guidance and restraint, what Welty's mother granted Eudora so fearfully and reluctantly—the freedom to develop in her own way as an artist in the wicked and dangerous outside world—Carson's mother seems almost to have urged upon her daughter. At seventeen Carson left home for New York.

The succeeding months of being "loose" in New York, moving about and supporting herself with odd jobs, undoubtedly fed her sense of loneliness. And her morbid imagination, her sense of the frailty and tenuousness of life and love, was deepened by her battle with serious illness that began when she was fifteen: rheumatic fever, heart disease, a cerebral vascular accident, breast cancer, a gradual deterioration of the body, and after a final massive stroke, death when she was fifty. These chronic afflictions were aggravated by chain smoking and heavy drinking.

McCullers's formal education extended only through high school, and though she became an avid reader of modern fiction, especially the great Russian novelists, her fiction shows little of the kind of encoded language, the biblical, classical, or romantic allusions to be found in the fiction of Porter and Welty. Carr describes her as having been "steeped" in Freud (39), which may partially account for her liberated attitudes about sex. However, Carson's sixteen-year marriage to Reeves McCullers, a sensitive and intelligent but ineffectual young man who shared his wife's aspiration to be a writer, as well as her bisexuality (they once fell in love with the same man), obviously affected her fictional portrayal of love. The marriage was romantic but stormy, competitive, and largely miserable, falling into a pattern of quarrels, separations (including a divorce), and reconciliations. There were suicide attempts, and Reeves finally shot himself in a state of despair.

Throughout her life, Carr shows, McCullers developed infatuations for persons of both genders, though rarely was her love returned in kind or intensity. No more than Porter does she seem to have been chiefly interested in the sexual relationship, which served mostly as a route to the intimacy and adoration both women craved. Though any deeply sympathetic person, like a psychiatrist, could unleash a surge of confessional love in her, McCullers's crushes seem usually to have been inspired by artistic talent, and she apparently conceived such a passion for Katherine Anne Porter when both writers were at Yaddo, the artist's colony in Saratoga Springs. Carr describes how, in the summer of 1941, Carson laid siege to Katherine Anne, following her around adoringly saying, "'I love you, Katherine Anne' ... with unabashed candor" (155). Once she is supposed to have "sprawled across the threshold" of Porter's door in an effort to see and talk to her, but Porter "merely stepped over her and continued on [her] way to dinner" (156), disliking lesbians, and feeling an especially strong antipathy for the strange young woman who so idolized her.

The question of sexual identity is crucial in McCullers's fiction, which often takes place in some unsettled no-man's land, nor woman's either. Yet her most successful work deals with the one period in the life of most people when sexuality is ambiguous, "in solution," so to speak—that of early adolescence. Because sexual ambivalence—with all its attendant yearnings, anxieties, explorations, idealism, hopes and despairs—is all but universal in that brief moment out of a life span, McCullers achieves her most convincing and appealing heroines in Mick Kelly of *The Heart is a Lonely Hunter* and Frankie Addams of *The Member of the Wedding*.

McCullers presents homosexual yearning, attachments, and frustrations with great sympathy and insight, especially in the characters of John Singer and Biff Brannon in *The Heart is a Lonely Hunter*. No doubt partly because these relationships were then widely regarded as pathological, partly because of McCullers's embracing of alienation, homosexuals are made to appear freakish or miserable in their attachments, which are neither reciprocal nor, for any length of time, fulfilling. The kind, all-absorbing Singer is a deaf-mute whose love for Spiros Anatonopoulous is thwarted from lack of response; and Cousin Lymon of *The Ballad of the Sad Café* is a hunchbacked dwarf scorned by the man he loves. The loves of that strange, circular round of lovers in *Ballad* seem to break with definite psychosexual labels. Miss Amelia is like a grown-up tomboy, though more male than female in her assumed sexual roles; and Marvin Macy, adored by Cousin Lymon, wants Miss Amelia only because she does not make the easy target he has made of the soft country girls he has left in the path of his destructive sexual relationships. He seems embattled with another man of strength superior to his. By allowing for the possibility of a sexual relationship between Miss Amelia and Cousin Lymon, McCullers gives the story another grotesque twist.

If the theme of the quest for sexual identity lends itself to modern psychological terms, McCullers's projection of that yearning of the self for completion in the other, what Frankie calls "the we of me," lends itself to more ancient mythical terms—to the view of love presented in Plato's *Symposium*, within a social and historical context of homosexuality. In that dialogue the view is presented, first by Aristophanes, that originally three sexes existed rather than two, the third being that of the hermaphrodite. These wonderfully furnished creatures (McCullers might have called them "finished") constituted a threat to the gods in their strength and pride. Socrates explains how Zeus executed the plan of cutting each of them in two, which accounts for the three varieties of sexual orientation. Love is the desire and pursuit of the whole. Whenever a half-lover has the good fortune, after long search, to encounter his or her other half, he or she experiences an ecstasy of fulfillment.

Something of this eager, tireless search of the split pairs of Plato's myth seems to drive both Carson and her characters, for the heart is a lonely hunter, and seeks that form of access to love that is communication. Plato tends to idealize homosexual love, especially when the sexual passion was mastered heroically through strength of mind and will and purity of spirit (illustrated by Socrates). This discipline freed the soul to ascend through the various stages of love, a love that led to the only valid form of immortality, through the mystical vision of God.

McCullers's ethos of love does not include such Platonic reaches, though she does show these strange loves of hers as attended by a beneficent overflow. The selfless, sympathetic presence of Singer, though uncomprehending and mute, is absorbent of much human need and frustration. Yet his capacity for receiving is dependent upon his own private escape hatch, in the form of the fat, nonabsorbent presence of his beloved Spiros, a narcissist who seems to live only to eat. Singer can no longer live when Spiros dies; his own despair and suicide result in the cutting of the lines of imagined communication with the four persons who use him as a confidante. As for Miss Amelia's love for Cousin Lymon, at first it leads wonderfully to the flowering of the sad café. There is an abundance of sociability: Cousin Lymon enjoys his new role as king of conversation and commander of the once penurious Miss Amelia, now dispenser of largess; her liquor flows freely, she applies her healing arts to the needy, especially children, and many a timid or shrunken soul emerges from hiding in the pleasurable ambiance of the café in its happy phase. But these loves are as vulnerable and ill-fated as the romantic attachments of Porter's characters, as much subject to destructive jealousy and hatred; and after the terrible fight between Marvin Macy and Miss Amelia, with her crushing defeat brought on by the decisive weight of Cousin Lymon, the café becomes once more, and this time permanently, the sad café.

The circle of loves in McCullers's fiction is always short-circuited, whether as result or source of the theory she imposes on the nature and functioning of love. In her own voice as narrator, she sets this theory forth at length in *The Ballad of the Sad Café*:

> First of all, love is a joint experience ... but it is [not] a similar experience to the two people involved.... The lover and the beloved ... come from different countries. Often the beloved is only a stimulus for all the stored-up love which has lain quiet within the lover for a long time hitherto.... He must create for himself a whole new inward world ... intense and strange.... The most outlandish people can be the stimulus for love.... A most mediocre person can be the object of a love which is wild, extravagant, and beautiful as the poison lilies of the swamp. A good man may be the stimulus for a love both violent and debased, or a jabbering madman may bring about in the soul of someone a tender and simple idyll. Therefore, the value and quality of any love is determined solely by the lover himself. It is for this reason that most of us would rather love than be loved.... The beloved fears and hates the lover.... For [he] is forever trying to strip bare his beloved. The lover craves any possible relation with the beloved, even if this experience can cause him only pain. (*Ballad* 26–27)

These theories have a ring of truth for more than McCullers's characters in *Ballad*: they apply to adolescent lovers, whose passionate attachments are often entirely subjective, unexpressed, and completely out of touch with reality (like that of the young girl in Welty's "A Memory"); they apply to any person in the grip of a compulsive attachment that is unreciprocated and may be masochistic; they doubtless applied to many of McCullers's own attachments. But they do not apply to the love relationships of most mature adults. Being so unrealistically founded, one-sided, and often grotesque, the love of McCullers's fictional characters is inevitably thwarted, leading to bitterness and defeat rather than the nobility of character so highly valued in Plato.

In an essay titled "The Flowering Dream: Notes on Writing" in *The*

Mortgaged Heart, McCullers has this to say about *Ballad*: "The passionate, individual love—the old Tristan–Isolde love, the Eros love—is inferior to the love of God, to fellowship, to the love of Agape—the Greek god of the feast, the God of brotherly love—and of man. This is what I tried to show in *The Ballad of the Sad Café* in the strange love of Miss Amelia for the little hunchback, Cousin Lymon" (281). The explanation is unclear, but perhaps McCullers means that in Miss Amelia's love and its beneficent effect on the café, McCullers was trying to present some merging of Greek and Christian love, as did Welty in *Delta Wedding*. In each case, generous impulses seem to be at work: a highly personal, nondoctrinaire love ethos that includes and embraces all sorts and conditions of men and women, rejoicing in all sorts of love feasts.

One can only guess the extent to which McCullers's views on love were shaped by her own bisexuality and then-current attitudes toward it. She cultivated and almost seemed to enjoy the idea of being a "freak" and the special outrage as well as the special sympathy that it evoked. Had she lived and written in the present era, she might have been able to imagine and project in fiction a love both reciprocal and mature, whether homosexual or heterosexual, but that does not seem likely. In temperament, she was too much the child, always retaining her childlike ways, and she appears to have been most content with mothering, sheltering figures who prized and adored her, such as her mother Marguerite, Tennessee Williams, Mary Mercer (a psychiatrist, McCullers's therapist and life-long friend), and Ida Reeder (her black housekeeper, nurse, secretary, and close companion in the last decade of McCullers's life). She remained always, as Tennessee Williams once described her in a poem, "the little boy ... with sorrows older than Naishapur" (Carr 537), the mysterious half child, half adult, always in search of another part of a divided self who never appeared.

Tracing the components of the love ethos of the three writers—childhood experience, personal "love life," reading and observation—we find much contrast and paradox. Porter's childhood was blighted by early loss of her mother, neglect of her father, strict rearing of a Methodist grandmother, poverty, ugliness, confinement of surroundings. She escaped through fantasy and an adventuresome, bohemian way of life. Callie renamed herself Katherine Anne and gave her fictional counterpart, Miranda, an aristocratic, slaveholding Catholic family with a romantic, chivalrous past. Welty's childhood was happy and carefree, sheltered in middle-class comfort by loving, nurturing parents within the codes of small-town Southern morality. She found her love models right within her family. McCullers's childhood was marked by the influence of an unconventional, strongly dominating mother who was convinced that her daughter was born to greatness. Carson adopted this notion, with the modification that she was also a freak, and therefore lonely, alienated, excluded from the support of human community while enabled by the perils and potentials of her gifts.

Porter's love life was a long history of largely disastrous marriages and affairs resulting in a paradoxical attitude of disillusionment about romantic and sexual passion together with a desire for it that often seems more like a compulsion or addiction than a perennial hope or idealism, though both of those qualities are to be found in the early, romantic stages of her affairs. Welty's early love life appears to have been very much like her family life—"normal" for an unusually imaginative, impressionable young woman—but we know little about it because of her insistence on privacy. McCullers's love life was blighted by a rocky marriage to a weak and competitive husband who only aggravated her own neurotic tendencies. For her as for Porter, love seems to have been to a great extent compulsive, causing her to "fall" for men and women who seemed to complete her own unfinished self. The paradox in these relationships was that by throwing herself slavishly at this strong, independent, artistic type of person she was all but insuring her rejection.

Books do not appear to have been as central to Porter and McCullers as they were to Welty, an inveterate and omnivorous reader from her earliest years. Fairy tales, myths, legends, the great works of fiction—all these were nutrients to the rich soil of her imagination and the development of her love ethos, as was her more extensive formal education. Welty also showed greater powers of empathy and imagination than the other two, who usually wrote more limitedly from their own immediate experience.

In quite different ways, I would regard both Porter and Welty as having "completed" love stories, both in and out of their fiction, whereas McCullers's personal story seems to fall short of completion. Her husband died a suicide; she seems never to have achieved much joy in her marriage nor other love attachments; her theory of love—lonely, unreciprocated, and incapable of durance—made it hopeless. She seemed as craving of attention, of gifts and all tangible signs of affection, as a child. Her life was continually afflicted by illness and terminated in early death; her last novel, *Clock Without Hands*, was unfinished and should probably not have been published.

McCullers not only seems "unfinished" in her personal life but also in her fictional theorizing about it seems never to have changed, developed, or even imagined some avatar of an ideal love, as did Porter and Welty. Late in her life, in ill health, she participated in an international symposium on "Sex in Literature" at the Cheltenham Literary Festival in England. Her contribution was to read, with great difficulty, her love thesis from *Ballad*, and the coda of the chain gang (Carr 517). To love irrationally and obsessively without hope of return, to fear and resist being the object of such love, to assuage grief and alienation by becoming a member of some real or imagined intimate group: she never envisioned beyond that poignancy.

Porter's life, extending into her nineties, seems to me a classic example of what is known as the self-fulfilling destiny. For all her misery, she got what she wanted: love, glamor, literary success, fame, and wealth. She became a legend. In one of her lovers she found an adoring, discriminating, emotionally stable man sympathetic to her nature and appreciative as well as supportive of her art—an ideal husband. But too late, she learned he was already happily married. In her eighty-seventh year she found an adoring, reliable attendant and lover in a forty-seven-year-old retired naval officer; the relationship was romantic and affectionate but asexual. She created a fictional ideal of love for Miranda in a character named Adam, who died young. Through all these experiences she retained the essentials of the Catholic faith to which she had converted as an adult, however little she seems to have practiced it.

Of the three writers only Welty, from limited experience but rich imaginative powers, has created images of love in many stages and conditions, from first love to mature conjugal love. Her comic spirit has provided perspective and balance, an essential part of the warm, tolerant humanism evident in her love ethos. If at times confusion results from her attempts to fuse the classical love ethos (pagan, mythical) with the Christian (*agape*), in her last novel she does present a clear image of love's *durance*, its power to survive the tests of sickness and death, to maintain continuity in the memory of a survivor. The depth, variety, and authenticity of her fictional portrayals of love speak for the great power of story through the ages—fairy and folk tales, myth, fiction of all kinds to which Welty has always been addicted—to generate more stories. Her success also shows the power of observation and a fertile imagination to conceive what personal experience cannot alone supply.

None of the three writers was a domesticated wife or loyal mate, and none had children. For all three, the art of fiction was a care and a passion, a first and last love, the means through which they tested their integrity. In that intense dedication they broke with the social codes that, in the South of their era, might have put them on a pedestal or made them slaves to their husbands and provided them narrowly circumscribed roles for developing their interests and talents. All three were masters of their craft; and thus, in and through their fiction, all three will live happily ever after.

WORKS CITED

Carr, Virginia S. *The Lonely Hunter*. Garden City, N.Y.: Doubleday, 1976.
Givner, Joan. *Katherine Anne Porter, a Life*. New York: Simon and Schuster, 1982.
McCullers, Carson. *The Ballad of the Sad Café*. New York: Bantam, 1969.

————. "The Flowering Dream: Notes on Writing." In *The Mortgaged Heart*. Ed. Margarita G. Smith. Boston: Houghton Mifflin, 1971. 274–82.

Porter, Katherine Anne. *The Collected Stories of Katherine Anne Porter*. New York: Harcourt Brace Jovanovich, 1965.

————.*Ship of Fools*. Boston: Little, Brown, 1962.

Welty, Eudora. *The Collected Stories of Eudora Welty*. New York: Harcourt Brace Jovanovich, 1980.

————. *Delta Wedding*. New York: Harcourt Brace Jovanovich, 1946.

————. *The Eye of the Story: Selected Essays and Reviews*. New York: Random House, 1978.

————. *One Writer's Beginnings*. Cambridge: Harvard University Press, 1984.

MARGARET WHITT

From Eros to Agape:
Reconsidering the Chain Gang's Song in McCullers's "Ballad of the Sad Café"

Carson McCullers closes her "Ballad of the Sad Café" with the chain gang—"Just twelve mortal men, seven of them black and five of them white boys from this county. Just twelve mortal men who are together" (66)— singing out on the Forks Fall highway. Throughout her works, McCullers uses music as a substitute when the intensity of the moment is too powerful for words. In a conversation, McCullers stated clearly her awareness of the inequities that permeated her home region:

> There is a special guilt in [Southerners], a seeking for something had—and lost. It is a consciousness of guilt not fully knowable, or communicable. Southerners are the more lonely and spiritually estranged, I think, because we have lived so long in an artificial social system that we insisted was natural and right and just— when all along we knew it wasn't. (McGill 217)

At the end of the "Ballad," McCullers's literal integration of the singing chain gang in a segregated South is her way of conveying the message that this novella has less to do with Eros—the passionate, individual love that exists between humans and controls the actions of Miss Amelia, Cousin Lymon, and Marvin Macy—than with Agape, the brotherly love of God.

From *Studies in Short Fiction* 33, no. 1 (Winter 1996). © 1996 by Newberry College.

McCullers must have known from the world as it existed around her in Columbus, Georgia, in the first half of this century, that the chain gangs, those groups of men in black and white striped uniforms who worked the roadside swinging picks, digging ditches, laying pipes, picking up trash, were rare visual examples of integration in an otherwise segregated South. The irony that McCullers suggests through the men's song—that they must be chained to be together to find harmony—was not lost on her.

Although the Southern prison system was segregated, the chain gang from its inception was integrated. According to *Statistical Abstracts of the United States: 1951*, Georgia did not submit information about prisoners received or discharged between the years 1938–45 (141), although a 1946 government document (*Prisoners in State and Federal Prisons and Reformatories*) indicates that 50.3% of new felony convicts in the South were black (29). In Georgia, there were 1,062 white men to 1,710 black men received in the prison system during this year of statistical gathering (30). It is safe to conjecture that black men outnumbered white men on most chain gangs throughout the first half of the century.

In *My Memoirs of Georgia Politics*, Rebecca Felton relates many disturbing memories that date from the turn of the century, including the story of a black man who spent 15 years on a chain gang for stealing a shotgun, and that of a 12-year-old black boy who was given 12 years on the chain gang for borrowing a horse to go for a short ride (658). In the case of *Johnson v. Dye* (1949), an escaped black Georgia prisoner was held by a federal court because of the horror stories about inhumane treatment—"that it was the custom of the Georgia authorities to treat chain gang prisoners with persistent and deliberate brutality [and] that Negro prisoners were treated with a greater degree of brutality than white prisoners" (Goldfarb 373). Georgia authorities could offer no testimony to the contrary, and the runaway escaped extradition.

In a 1932 bestseller, Robert E. Burns, a white man, documented the treatment he experienced in his *I Am a Fugitive from a Georgia Chain Gang*, available during McCullers's teenage years in the Muscogee County Library in Columbus. A second book in that same year, John Spivak's *Georgia Nigger*, called the public's attention (and, in all likelihood, that of the 15-year-old McCullers) to the atrocities in McCullers's home state. Both books were widely reviewed with the aim of reforming the penal code. In *World Tomorrow*, E. Y. Webb notes that *Georgia Nigger* has "relatively few new facts brought to light here, [but it is] ... a picture ... more moving than studies and statistics" (428). Spivak tells his story through a fictionalized account of David's efforts "to escape from a monstrous system" (i). Especially disturbing in the Spivak book is a series of photographs of black men in their striped uniforms in the cage, the stocks, and on the rack. None looks as though he would be capable of joy in song.

McCullers captures the essence of the call-and-response method of discourse found in African-American church services: "One dark voice will start a phrase, half-sung, and like a question. And after a moment another voice will join in, soon the whole gang will be singing. The voices are dark in the golden glare, the music intricately blended, both somber and joyful" (66). But she is careful not to let the word "joyful" hang in the air. She qualifies the comment, trying to move toward a closer assessment of what the chain gang's song might mean: "It is music that causes the heart to broaden and the listener to grow cold with ecstasy and fright" (66). Her response to this music is similar to that of Frederick Douglass, who, in his *Narrative*, recounts the singing of the slaves on the way to the Great House Farm: "The hearing of those wild notes always depressed my spirit, and filled me with ineffable sadness" (31). When Douglass went to the North, he was stunned to hear that many thought the singing was "evidence of contentment and happiness" (32). "It is impossible to conceive of a greater mistake," he wrote. "Slaves sing most when they are most unhappy. The songs of the slave represent the sorrows of his heart; and he is relieved by them, only as an aching heart is relieved by its tears" (32). Douglass had the advantage of speaking as an insider; his words have the ring of credibility.

McCullers's rendering of the chain gang's song is not a picture of contentment, yet critic Ihab Hassan sees their song as summoning "the indestructible joy of endurance and transcendent pain" (226). Richard Cook joins Hassan in the use of "joy," suggesting the prisoners have "an elemental capacity for joy that transcends and changes, if only for a moment, the miserable conditions of their lives" (100). The implication that "joy" can come from physical degradation is disturbing. Can the reader be pacified by such a "joyful" interpretation, and thereby forgiven any "shared burden of Southern history," as C. Vann Woodward might call it? Can the reader, even for a brief and fleeting moment, believe that the chain gang member and contributor to song is, as Douglass says, doing anything more than expressing "the sorrows of his heart"? Virginia Spencer Carr's suggestion that "one's only relief" (59) is "to seek solace" (66) by listening to the chain gang slants McCullers's position. The author never posits that comfort will come from this activity; rather, walking down to the Forks Fall highway is something "you might as well" do (4, 65). Simply stated, there is no joy in this kind of enduring—for the convict, for the reader.

Not much happens in "Ballad" to soothe the wounded spirit in the love triangle of Miss Amelia to Cousin Lymon to Marvin Macy to Miss Amelia again. Their story, set within the frame of the singing chain gang down on the Forks Fall highway, is reflected onto a grander, more cosmic scope by the "twelve mortal men who are together." McCullers, by story's end, leaves the reader considering these questions: Are chains what it takes to bond black and white men together in the South? Is any kind of reciprocal love possible in such a universe? Can the only tie that binds humanity be inhumane suffering held in common?

The chain gang is the frame of the story, not a closing mysterious appendage. McCullers's elevation of love from Eros to Agape succeeds precisely by way of ironic failure. In the South, at the time she was writing, for black man and white man to produce the harmony that should prevail in a world where Agape is understood, she had to remove the song from the people and place it where it could make a stronger statement. The music had to "swell," and it had to be relocated to "the earth itself, or the wide sky" (66). The harmony that comes from and out of the world around us is how McCullers's vision transcends, how it pushes toward Agape. The reality, however, is "one lonely voice, ... the sun, the sound of the picks in the silence" (66). McCullers gives a perverse hope, disturbing enough to let that message in the chain gang's song reverberate: Must it be, always, "the sound of the picks" or are "twelve mortal men who are together," without the chains, possible in this specific geographic region? Beyond this place where the "soul rots with boredom" (65) is there something more? Not yet, McCullers is saying, but the chain gang's music does haunt the heart.

WORKS CITED

Burns, Robert E. *I Am a Fugitive from a Georgia Chain Gang*. n.p.: n.p., 1932.
Carr, Virginia Spencer. *Understanding Carson McCullers*. Columbia: U of South Carolina P, 1990.
Cook, Richard M. *Carson McCullers*. New York: Ungar, 1975,
Douglass, Frederick. *Narrative of the Life of Frederick Douglass: An American Slave*. New York: Signet, 1968.
Felton, Rebecca Latimer. *My Memoirs of Georgia Politics*. Atlanta: Index Printing, 1911.
Goldfarb, Ronald and Linda Singer. *After Conviction*. New York: Simon, 1973.
Hassan, Ihab. *Radical Innocence: The Contemporary American Novel*. New York: Harper, 1961.
McCullers, Carson. *The Ballad of the Sad Carl*. Boston: Houghton, 1951.
McGill, Ralph. *The South and the Southerner*. Boston: Little, 1963.
Spivak, John L. *Georgia Nigger*. Montclair, New Jersey: Patterson Smith, 1969.
US Bureau of the Census. *Prisoners in State and Federal Prisons and Reformatories*. Washington, DC: GPO, 1948.
———. *Statistical Abstract of the United States: 1951*. 72nd ed. Washington, DC: GPO, 1951.
Webb, E.Y. Rev. of *Georgia Nigger*. *World Tomorrow* 15 (2 Nov. 1932): 428.

CLARE WHATLING

Reading Miss Amelia:
critical strategies in the construction of
sex, gender, sexuality, the gothic and grotesque

REVOLTING FEMININITY

The plot of Carson McCullers's *The Ballad of the Sad Café* (1943)[1] revolves around the figure of Miss Amelia Evans, 'a cross-eyed, masculine giantess in overalls',[2] who at 6 feet 2 inches is described by Louis Auchincloss as 'the man-woman, the rich miser and business executive, taciturn, suspicious, misanthropic and terrified of sex'.[3] An early passage in *The Ballad of the Sad Café* testifies to the complexity of Miss Amelia's negotiation of socially inscribed notions of sex and gender: 'She was a dark, tall woman with bones and muscles like a man. Her hair was cut short and brushed back from the forehead, and there was about her sunburned face a tense, haggard quality. She might have been a handsome woman if, even then, she was not slightly cross-eyed' (8). The physiological distinction which marks Amelia as different, that is her unusual height and musculature, is noted by the townspeople, who deem her height 'not natural for a woman' (20). It is made clear, however, that Amelia's physical strangeness is exaggerated only when she attempts to conform to feminine norms. For example, we are told that Amelia looks odd in a dress which 'hung on her in a most peculiar fashion' (31). Thus a physiological and social norm is invoked, by which terms Amelia fails. In dungarees, on the contrary, Amelia is shown to be at ease, their careless androgyny allowing her to move easily and forget the social

From *Modernist Sexualities*, edited by Hugh Stevens and Caroline Howlett. © 2000 by Manchester University Press.

limitations of her sex. Indeed, exhibiting a refreshing insouciance in the face of gender conventions, Amelia pays scant attention to conventional notions of feminine etiquette: 'Miss Amelia ate slowly and with the relish of a farmhand. She ate with both elbows on the table, bent over the plate, her knees spread wide apart and her feet braced on the rungs of the chair' (16–17). Infringing class as well as gender expectations, Amelia is hardly the conventional picture of the southern heiress. Indeed, her habits are rarely ladylike: 'Having finished, Miss Amelia tilted back her chair, tightened her fist, and felt the hard, supple muscles of her right arm beneath the clean, blue cloth of her shirtsleeves—an unconscious habit with her at the close of the meal' (17). Miss Amelia is a woman who takes pride in the exhibition of her musculature, and the unconsciousness of her actions are, it is implied, a result of her upbringing—as the only daughter to a man who brought her up, motherless and like a son. Her inheritance of her daddy's store, fields and whisky still accounts for and justifies this upbringing in the sense that, as Margaret Bolsteri notes, the power that accrues to Amelia as richest person in the town puts her 'beyond public opinion'.[4]

To add to the complexity of her characterisation, the narrator makes it clear that Amelia's unusual stance does not render her unattractive to men: 'There were those who would have courted her' (8–9) remarks the story's narrator. However, as the narrator also warns: 'Miss Amelia cared nothing for the love of men' (9). Her reputation for incalculability is only confirmed by her ten-day marriage to the local Don Juan, Marvin Macy. Marrying Macy, it is assumed, for his money, Amelia ousts him from the marriage bed and later sees him off her land at the point of a gun. It was, remarks the narrator, 'a strange and dangerous marriage, lasting only ten days, that left the whole town wondering and shocked' (9).

McCullers's Miss Amelia has puzzled, perturbed and haunted readers since the book's appearance. Ambiguous of appearance and intent, Amelia continues to fascinate by the very fact that she confounds conventional sex and gender categorisation. This has not, however, prevented critics from trying to delimit her to one, usually pejorative, definition or another. Indeed, the critical reception of Amelia has been marked by a degree of distaste which seems, at the very least, unusual. Louis Auchincloss's 1961 description of Amelia as a man-woman points to the definitional ambiguity at the heart of her reception. Other critics are less open in their reading of Amelia. To William Peden, for example, Amelia is 'grotesque, freakish, incongruous',[5] while to Chester Eisinger she becomes 'bizarre, lonely, hermaphroditic'.[6] Gender ambiguity thus provokes questions regarding Amelia's anatomical status. Even in the 1970s avowedly feminist critic Louise Westling displays a fascinating degree of anxiety when trying to account for Amelia. For

Westling *The Ballad of the Sad Café* 'is a nightmare vision of the tomboy grown up, without any concessions to social demands for sexual conformity'.[7] McCullers's representation of Amelia as a: 'grotesque extreme of masculinity'[8] leads Westling to term the character 'monstrous' and a 'freak'.[9] Even a rare contemporary, and for a change, sympathetic, reading of the novella, plots Amelia's gender ambiguity as a 'frightening prophecy for readers unwilling to cooperate with the return to a masculinist economy after the [second world] war'.[10] Such critical posturing demonstrates the challenge Amelia poses, a definitional ambivalence which leads me to situate the contradictions posed by McCullers's character within the style commonly known as the grotesque.

As Peter Thomson observes, 'What is grotesque to one person may be only bizarre to another.'[11] Hence a concept of the grotesque first requires a conceiver. Within a specifically American context we might of course cite Sherwood Anderson's equation of the grotesque with the deformation of an idea to the point of obsession, an area developed in his novel *Winesberg, Ohio*.[12] This is a trope which is employed also in the work of McCullers's contemporary Flannery O'Connor,[13] and arguably influences the work of that candid charter of southern gothic malaise, Tennessee Williams. It is to McCullers's predecessor Djuna Barnes that we might turn, however, if we are to get closer to the source of McCullers's negotiation of the grotesque. For it is in works like *Ryder, Nightwood* and *The Book of Repulsive Women*[14] that we discover the true precursors to McCullers's Miss Amelia, women (and men) who fly in the face of social convention, engendered from the mind of a woman who celebrates the inverse over the norm.[15] Indeed, it is in Barnes's writings that we recognise a like representation of the hybrid, the outsider and the 'monster' treated with a sympathy that, as Jane Marcus puts it, 'mothers the Other'.[16]

To most critics Amelia is grotesque because she transgresses conventional boundaries, presenting a bizarre mix of sex and gender characteristics. For Peter Thomson the grotesque is something which 'involves the body in a quite direct way' in that it is the '*physical* nature of the ... descriptions presented—physical in ... an immediate and vivid way'[17] that truly disturbs. Departing from this point, my contention is that what offends readers about Miss Amelia is her *visible* manifestation of gender mix, and *what remains invisible*, the question—or not—of her anatomical difference. On this matter we are teased mercilessly by the author. Here for example is McCullers's description of Amelia by the fire, an image which engenders both curiosity and anxiety:

> She did not warm her backside modestly, lifting her skirt only an
> inch or so, as do most women in public. There was not a grain of

> modesty about Miss Amelia, and she frequently seemed to forget
> altogether that there were men in the room. Now as she stood
> warming herself, her red dress was pulled up quite high in the
> back so that a piece of her strong hairy thigh could be seen by
> anyone who cared to look at it. (71)

And of course we do care to look, for we are fascinated as well as alienated
by the contradictory nature of this vision.[18] For the visual mix of socially
inscribed gender (the hairiness of the thigh, the lack of feminine modesty) is
underlined by an insistent worry as to what lies above the strong hairy thigh.
Leslie Fiedler notes how traditionally excess of body hair is thought to
denote excessive genitalia.[19] And indeed I would argue it is in this image of
Amelia that critical anxiety around Amelia's sex (anatomy), sexuality
(orientation) and gender (a visible manifestation of masculinity presupposing
a questioning of anatomy and orientation) accumulate. Amelia offends both
in her visibility (the exhibition of hairy muscular thighs) and in what remains
unseen, for what she fails to reveal but suggests. Hence I would argue that
the grotesque in the *Ballad* functions around 'what is visually obscure, but
demands to be seen'.[20] The possibility as to what Amelia may be hiding
beneath her red dress fascinates but also repulses. What we *witness* in Amelia
is an objective display of masculine style. What we *imagine* is the translation
of behaviour into morphology. The story plays on this ambiguity but gives
no answer, leaving the reader with a sense of 'conflicts unresolved',[21] a
notion which perhaps lies at the heart of the grotesque. It is thus what
readers add to Amelia in their imagination that renders Amelia grotesque.
Our fear imagines its own horrors.

Whilst playing upon the fantasies of her readers, however, it must be
pointed out that McCullers does not herself seek to pathologise Amelia in
any way. Indeed, her narrator's tone reads as almost blasé in passages such as
the one above, as if delighting in the consternation it engenders while
pretending a sense of studied insouciance.[22] Most telling is McCullers's
avoidance of the sexological discourse which Amelia's physiology tends to
provoke in others. Amelia is of course classically 'inverse' in her exhibition of
masculine style and behaviour, yet McCullers refuses to draw the appropriate
cultural conclusions.[23] This is far from the case with McCullers' critical
readers, however, who, are quick to turn ambiguity into condemnation.
Roger Gray, for example argues that: 'By reducing her appearance to a series
of conflicting angles, by emphasizing her physical defects and her
masculinity (or rather, her sexual ambivalence), McCullers effectively
transforms Miss Amelia into a freak.'[24] As Jana Sawicki, discussing
Foucauldian understandings of deviancy, notes: 'Foucault claims that

deviancy is controlled and norms established through the very process of identifying deviant activity as such, then observing it, further classifying it, and monitoring and "treating" it.'[25] Deviance is then less a natural fact than a social production and is always relative to the standard which is posited in a given society as the norm.[26] As Jonathan Dollimore characterises this movement:

> This much has become certain: deviancy isn't just a waste product of society, and nor is it intrinsic to the deviant subject. It is, rather, a construction, one which when analysed, says less and less about the individual deviant and more and more about the society—its structures of power, representation and repression— identifying or demonising him or her.[27]

Hence, what is rendered deviant within any society finally comes to be as significant as that which has been retained and normalised.

The idea of a specifically sexual deviance is often invoked in contemplation of Miss Amelia. Indeed, in the literary reception of McCullers's work from the mid 1950s it becomes something of a critical trope. In a review of the Edward Albee stage adaptation of the novella, Robert Brustein refers to Amelia as 'a dwarf loving lesbian' and a 'bull dyke'.[28] Both, in the context of his writing, are terms of denigration. What is particularly interesting to me about this construction of deviance, however, is the link which is made between it and the literary tradition of the gothic. Here, for example, Robert Phillips, in characterising McCullers's corpus, observes: 'It is clear that the work of Carson McCullers belongs within that body of our literature which is Gothic in theme and method. Instead of romantic couples or brave heroes or heroines we find homosexuals and lesbians, flowers of evil dotting a grotesque landscape.'[29] Phillips' point is developed by critic Leslie Fiedler, who adds a new element to the condemnation, the notion of degeneration. For Fiedler, McCullers's writing spells the last death rattle of a southern gothic tradition which had seen its apotheosis in the work of William Faulkner. This is a tradition now in decline, and the deadly virus which ushers in the decline of the once proud Faulknerian tradition is, according to Fiedler, gender. The 'feminising Faulknerians'[30] have given new life to the gothic, but they have also taken something away from it. This lack, it is evident from Fiedler's argument, is masculinity: 'manliness'.[31] Women writers have at the same time added two typically feminine elements to the genre: 'decadence' and 'preciousness'.[32] It is unsurprising then that the element soon to be introduced into Fiedler's argument is homosexuality, since the association between femininity, effeminacy and homosexuality is a long and established one.[33] These new gothic texts are, Fiedler claims, 'quite frankly homosexual'.[34] Indeed in Fiedler's argument the gothic operates as a means of coding, of rendering covert, the inadmissible. For despite a detente in social attitudes towards homosexuality, the subject, he feels, still requires a discreet handling and this is what the gothic effects through the metaphorical revelation of its subject matter.[35] One consequence of this, however, is the degeneration of the gothic in style and form.

THE GOTHIC HOMOSEXUAL

Generic definitions are always problematic, and any attempt to define the American gothic tradition at this point no less so than usual. The 'gothic novel proper',[36] as Eve Sedgwick terms it, can easily be traced in terms of lineage and theme to late eighteenth-century England and the classic gothic romances of Mrs Radcliffe and 'Monk' Lewis. The term's more recent application to twentieth-century southern American fiction is more open to contention, and its suitability is even questioned by some.[37] Indeed, it must be said that its transformation, even in tracing a lineage through Hawthorne and Poe, is considerable. Though comparative studies do exist, my own consideration of the southern gothic will not encompass these since I am less interested in tracing a history or lineage than in the positing of effects and the gauging of reader response. *The Ballad of the Sad Café's* relation to a wider gothic tradition interests me only as it reflects upon this reception, and on the whole I am happy to have the term gothic remain provisional (as all terms must) in its application to McCullers's work.

Having noted the provisional nature of literary definitions, I will, however, introduce this section by isolating a few obviously gothic elements in McCullers's fiction. Eve Sedgwick's characterisation of gothic properties may sound familiar to readers of *The Ballad*:

> [S]ubterranean spaces and live burial; doubles; the discovery of obscured family ties [Lymon's tenuous claim of kinship with Amelia] ... possibilities of incest [the horrified speculation of the town gossips that relations between the two have become sexual] ... the unspeakable ... the poisonous effects of guilt and shame; nocturnal landscapes and dreams; apparitions from the past [the return of Marvin Macy]; Faust—and Wandering-Jew like figures [Lymon again]; civil insurrections and fires.[38]

Following this tradition, *The Ballad* opens in characteristic southern gothic style with the now classic description of the ghost town:

> The town itself is dreary; not much is there except the cotton mill, the two-room houses where the workers live, a few peach trees, a church with two coloured windows, and a miserable main street only a hundred yards long ... Otherwise the town is lonesome, sad, and like a place that is far off and estranged from all other places in the world. (7)

Boredom, decay and a sense of hopelessness dominate this description. Like the castles of the Italian Renaissance which form the background to the classical gothic of Radcliffe and Lewis, the town is removed from civilisation, escape is impossible. The introduction then sets the scene for the gothic focus proper, the broken-down old house at the centre of the town:

> The largest building in the very center of the town is boarded up completely ... The building looks completely deserted. Nevertheless, on the second floor there is one window which is not boarded; sometimes in the late afternoon when the heat is at its worst a hand will slowly open the shutter and a face will look down on the town. (7)

Deserted buildings that have seen better times, a breathless air of mysteries to be unfolded, dislocated bodies caught in the shadow of windows: we recognise each element as distinctively gothic.

Where, however, is the homosexual, argued by critics to be such a central theme of the genre? Surely, if homosexuality is anywhere it must be located in the haunted occupier of the derelict town store, Miss Amelia Evans? Perhaps the link which David Punter makes between the gothic and the 'questioning of the absolute nature of sex roles'[39] will help us here. For Miss Amelia, as I have noted, is tall, masculine and independent. Her physical and social display of gender difference leads readers to question her sexual status. Is she a woman, is she a man, is she, as Robert Brustein claims, a lesbian? Does McCullers's creation of a character who questions traditional sex and gender roles, in other words, render Amelia homosexual? Certainly a preference for masculine dress and role can and does stand as one signification of lesbianism. On the other hand a working definition of a lesbian might be a woman whose erotic focus is towards her own sex. Yet when we apply this definition to Amelia we find it to be insufficient. Amelia has almost no communication with the other women within the story and appears to show no interest in them, even at the story's end refusing the townswomen's offers to help clear up the wreckage left by Lymon and Macy. Moreover, her only love focus is heterosexual—for the hunchback but none the less male Cousin Lymon. Of course this is where critics become entangled because of the complex web of gender and sex relations this union prefigures. It is therefore worth spending some time now extracting its elements.

The beginning of the story finds Amelia introverted and morose, distributing whisky to shamefaced townsmen. It is at this point, however, that love touches Amelia in the shape of the 4-foot-tall hunchback Cousin Lymon who arrives in town that night claiming kinship with the irascible miser. This love, though at first viewed by the townspeople as grotesquely inappropriate, reforms Amelia, who in indulging Lymon becomes a positive, facilitating force in the town. She achieves this in part by setting up at Lymon's instigation a café, which becomes the town's focal point and chief entertainment. The former misanthrope cannot now do enough for her love, bestowing gift upon gift, giving over every inch of her livelihood to the mysterious Lymon. It is this love which becomes the focus of consternation and speculation for the townspeople of the *Ballad*.

As I have described, Amelia is a woman who is characterised as masculine in appearance and behaviour. Lymon on the other hand is represented as an emasculated figure who in the course of the story cries, gossips, dances and flutters his eyelids, all characteristics associated with a conventional construction of femininity. He is further feminised in his relation to Amelia through the association of femininity with narcissism: 'Each night the hunchback came down the stairs with the air of one who has a grand opinion of himself. He always smelled slightly of turnip greens, as Miss Amelia rubbed him night and morning with pot liquor to give him strength. She spoiled him to a point beyond reason' (30–1). In this description we recognise the inverted dynamics of the love relation in which these two are engaged as we see Amelia taking on what is essentially the part of the wooer, supplicating herself before the needs of her beloved. Hence it is Amelia who performs the function of the chivalrous gallant, carrying Lymon across river and through swamp. It is she who buys a car out of her own funds and who transports Lymon across country in search of treats to entertain. In performing these tasks Amelia is firmly positioned in the role of courtly lover, obedient, idealising, courteous and ultimately abject: 'Grotesque though it might seem Amelia is in fact the archetype of the romantic lover, and the fact that the object of her love is unworthy of it makes her not the less typical, but the more so, since idealization is the essence of romantic love.'[40] In all, the consideration with which she treats his aches and agues and the conciliation she applies to his discontents position Amelia as faithful retainer to Lymon's southern belle—a performance he maintains even to the traditional descent from the staircase. In short, Lymon takes up the traditionally feminine role as (s)he who is wooed, with Amelia in the masculine role as wooer. What we have as a result is a kind of inverse, indeed even transvestite, heterosexuality, which is normal in its pairings—a man and a woman are involved—but abnormal in its individual dynamics in that the woman takes on the man's role and the man the woman's. What we witness, accordingly, is a deformation of the heterosexual norm into a grotesque parody of itself. Hence, I would suspect, the anxiety of the critics before this relation since what we come to see is that it is heterosexuality that is distorted within the story, not as homosexuality but *as* heterosexuality.

Yet this is not the only way one can read this relation. For a start, might not Amelia's wooing of Lymon be read not merely as a grotesque parody of heterosexuality, but in line with recent theories of performativity,[41] as a parody of a parody, namely as butch-femme lesbian role play with Amelia performing the butch to Lymon's femme? The resurgence of the homosexual possibility between the two can be taken further, however. For example, might not the butch-femme exchange between them be read just as easily as male homosexual[42] as lesbian, since just as Amelia is a woman performing masculinity to Lymon's male femme, so Lymon is a man performing femininity to Amelia's butch? This is certainly a dynamic one could pursue in characterising the relation between Lymon and the hypermasculine Marvin Macy where Lymon femmes it up with regard to Macy's butch indifference.[43] And if one is homosexualising the relation between Lymon and Macy, why not pursue the connotations of Macy's obsession with the masculine Amelia? Chased off his own land through the barrel of a gun, certainly Macy too can be feminised in relation to his phallic bride of nine days. With such potentially complex readings of the triangular relations being played out through the novella it seems difficult to plot what form of sexual desire is being prioritised in the triangle, or indeed whether any one form is being prioritised at all. All the more pertinent then, that the critical reception of the *Ballad* has sought to confine the source of sex and gender ambiguity in the novella to the figure of Miss Amelia. It is for this reason, then, that whilst recognising the productive possibilities in figuring the relations between Amelia and Lymon, Lymon and Macy, or Macy and Amelia as homosexual, my preferred reading of the novella pursues what I argue to be McCullers's radical deconstruction of compulsory heterosexuality as inverse grotesque. It is to this reading, therefore, that I now return.

Peter Thomson argues that 'The effect of the grotesque can best be

HARPER COLLEGE LIBRARY
PALATINE, ILLINOIS 60067

summed up as alienation. Something which is familiar is suddenly made
strange and disturbing.'[44] The similarity of Thomson's description to
Freud's notion of the *unheimlich* (the 'uncanny') seems pertinent. In Freud's
argument the *heimlich*, that which is familiar, known of old, homely, contains
within its etymology, though as its inverse, the term *unheimlich*, meaning
'eerie, weird, arousing, gruesome'.[45] A relation between these two categories
is always implicit: 'What is *heimlich* comes to be *unheimlich*.'[46] For Freud the
uncanny is 'that class of the frightening which leads back to something which
is known of old and long familiar'.[47] The similarity in turn of these
definitions to McCullers's transposition should be clear. For in McCullers's
story it is heterosexuality, the known quantity, that is rendered unfamiliar,
grotesque, by its reconfiguration into the inverse heterosexuality of Lymon
and Amelia. Like the hideous shape of Lymon and Amelia on the staircase,
what this prefigures is the terrifying possibility of their heterosexual
conjunction: 'Miss Amelia walked slowly, two steps at a time, holding the
lamp high. The hunchback hovered so close behind her that the swinging
light made on the staircase wall one great, twisted shadow of the two of them'
(17). The distortion of courtly conventions precipitates the cultural
insinuation of the beast with two backs, an image which McCullers plays
upon in her description of the shadowy bodies on the wall. Indeed, it is at this
point that the speculation concerning the couple's physical relations ensues:

> [A]ccording to Mrs McPhail, a warty-nosed old busybody who is
> continually moving her sticks of furniture from one part of the
> room to another; according to her and certain others, these two
> were living in sin. If they were related, they were only a cross
> between first and second cousins, and even that could in no way
> be proved. Now, of course, Miss Amelia was a powerfully
> blunderbuss of a person, more than six feet tall—and Cousin
> Lymon a weakly little hunchback reaching only to her waist. But
> so much the better for Mrs Stumpy McPhail and her cronies, for
> they and their kind glory in conjunctions which are ill-matched
> and pitiful. (32)

It is thus, to reaffirm, heterosexuality that is rendered grotesque within the
Ballad, structured within the inverse dynamics of Amelia and Lymon's
'queer', but ultimately 'straight' relation.

Following Eve Sedgwick I would argue that the association
gothic–degeneracy–homosexuality formulated by Fiedler, Phillips and others
is a homophobic one. The association is a product of the homophobia of a
critical hegemony which *requires* homosexuality to be rendered covertly

through the gothic form, and which *assumes* a self-evident correlation between homosexuality and degeneration. This construction of the gothic operates as a site of containment, delimiting meaning to one function. The gothic as employed by McCullers on the other hand can be read as a more open text. For in her work the gothic is deployed not as a veil to disguise homosexuality but as a device which promotes (hetero)sexual uncertainty and which leaves questions regarding a subject's sexual status unanswered. That it is heterosexuality that is rendered unfamiliar, grotesque, through its configurations in the relation between Amelia and Lymon seems to me, in the light of Amelia's negative critical reception, to be the most fruitful reading of the *Ballad*. What we see in the posturing of McCullers's critical readers is a compulsory heterosexual anxiety which encodes itself as a homophobic fear of difference, a difference which it encodes as gothic or grotesque. As I have argued, one of the aims of the social construction of deviance is to label certain social activities as deviant in order to normalise others. What McCullers does in my reading of her novella is to play on such critical anxieties, defamiliarising heterosexual conventions by rendering them as they are 'deformed' by her characters, inappropriate. In that compulsory heterosexuality is at the root of the distaste displayed in the critical reception of a character like Miss Amelia, what we thus see in the reception of McCullers's work is a heterosexual (homophobic) gothic masquerading as homosexual (deviant), while in McCullers's work, the site of contested sexuality is, in fact, straight.

NOTES

1. C. McCullers, *The Ballad of the Sad Café* (London, Penguin, 1963). All future references are given in the text.

2. K. Lubbers, 'The Necessary Order: A Study of Theme and Structure in Carson McCullers' Fiction', in H. Bloom, ed., *Carson McCullers* (London, Chelsea, 1986), pp. 33–52, p. 32.

3. L. Auchincloss, *Pioneers and Caretakers: A Study of American Women Novelists* (Minneapolis, University of Minnesota Press, 1961), p. 166.

4. M. Bolsteri, '"Bound" Characters in Porter, Welty and McCullers: The Pre-Revolutionary Status of Women in American Fiction', *Bucknell Review*, 24 (1978): 95–105, p. 104.

5. W. Peden, *The American Short Story* (Boston, Houghton Mifflin, 1964), p. 109.

6. C. Eisinger, *Fiction of the Forties* (Chicago, Chicago University Press, 1965), p. 245.

7. L. Westling, 'Carson McCullers' Tomboys', *Southern Humanities Review*, 14 (1980): 339–50, p. 345.

8. Westling, 'Carson McCullers' Tomboys', p. 245.

9. L. Westling, 'Carson McCullers' Amazon Nightmare', *Modern Fiction Studies*, 28 (1982) 465–73, p. 465.

10. C. Hannon, '"The Ballad of the Sad Café" and Other Stories of Women's Wartime Labor', in T. Foster, E. Siegel and L. Berry, eds., *Bodies in Writing, Bodies in Performance* (New York, New York University Press, 1996).

11. P. Thomson, *The Grotesque* (London, Methuen, 1972), p. 32.

12. S. Anderson, *Winesburg, Ohio* (New York, Viking Press, 1966).

13. O'Connor's *Wise Blood* (New York, Farrar, Straus and Giroux, 1962) certainly charts the progression of obsession into pathology.

14. D. Barnes, *Ryder* (New York, St Martin's Press, 1979), *Nightwood* (London, Faber, 1980), *The Book of Repulsive Women* (Los Angeles, Sun and Moon Press, 1989).

15. See, for example, S. Stephenson's reading of *Ryder*, 'Writing the Grotesque Body: Djuna Barnes' Carnival Parody', in M. Broe, ed., *Silence and Power: A Reevaluation of Djuna Barnes* (Carbondale, Southern Illinois University Press, 1989), pp. 81–91.

16. J. Marcus, 'Laughing at Leviticus: *Nightwood* as Woman's Circus Epic', in Broe, ed., *Silence and Power*, pp. 221–50, p. 228.

17. Thomson, *The Grotesque*, p. 8.

18. As Bakhtin observes: 'Displeasure is caused by the impossible and improbable nature of the image', M. Bakhtin, *Rabelais and His World*, trans. H. Iswolsky (Bloomington, Indiana University Press, 1984), p. 303. However, this displeasure remains in tension with the fascination in looking on, the desire to penetrate to the heart of the mystery almost, in a sense, despite oneself.

19. L. Fiedler, *Freaks* (New York, Simon and Schuster, 1978), p. 178.

20. C. Kahane, 'The Gothic Mirror', in S. N. Garner, C. Kahane and M. Sprengnether, eds., *The (M)Other Tongue: Essays in Feminist Psychoanalytic Interpretation* (Ithaca, Cornell University Press, 1985), pp. 334–51, p. 347.

21. *The Grotesque*, p. 21.

22. In this attitude too McCullers shares the breezy tone of Djuna Barnes, whose repulsive ladies sail through life oblivious to the consternation they engender in those of a less benign disposition.

23. Namely that Amelia is a lesbian. For a now classic reading of the invert, see S. Ruehl, 'Inverts and Experts: Radclyffe Hall and the Lesbian Identity', in R. Brunt and C. Rowan, eds., *Feminism, Culture and Politics* (London, Lawrence and Wishart, 1982). One can only speculate as to the reason behind McCullers's refusal to draw out the implication invert-lesbian. My preferred reading is to locate her refusal alongside what I will argue below to be her radical deconstruction of heterosexuality as a system which contains within itself the seeds of its own dissolution. Amelia, in other words, becomes all the more of a conundrum as her focus remains heterosexual (for the mysterious stranger Cousin Lymon), but skewed by her embracing of masculine gender characteristics.

24. R. Gray, 'Moods and Absences', in Bloom, ed., *Carson McCullers*, pp. 77–85, p. 81.

25. J. Sawicki, 'Identity Politics and Sexual Freedom', in I. Diamond and L. Quinby, eds., *Feminism and Foucault: Reflections on Resistance* (Boston, Northeastern University Press, 1988), pp. 177–91, pp. 182–3.

26. See Foucault's argument for the proliferation of deviant sexualities at the end of the eighteenth century, a development coterminous with the deployment of sexuality through multiple discourses of regulation and desire. M. Foucault, *The History of Sexuality: An Introduction*, trans. R. Hurley (London, Random House, 1978).

27. J. Dollimore, 'The Dominant and the Deviant: A Violent Dialectic', *Critical Quarterly*, 28 (1986): 179–92, pp. 182–3.

28. R. Brustein, *Seasons of Discontent* (New York, Simon and Schuster, 1965), p. 157.

29. R. Phillips, 'The Gothic Architecture of *The Member of the Wedding*', *Renascence*, 16 (1964): 59–72, p. 61.

30. L. Fiedler, *Love and Death in the American Novel* (New York, Dell, 1966), p. 449. In this term he includes the work of McCullers's near contemporaries Flannery O'Connor and Eudora Welty.

31. Fiedler, *Love and Death*, p. 449.

32. Fiedler, *Love and Death*, p. 450.

33. As Gayle Rubin argues: 'The suppression of the homosexual component of human sexuality, and by corollary, the oppression of homosexuality, is ... a product of the same system whose rules and relations oppress women.' G. Rubin, 'The Traffic in Women: Notes on the "Political Economy" of Sex', in R. Reiter, ed., *Toward an Anthropology of Women* (London, Monthly Review Press, 1975), pp. 157–210, p. 180.

34. Fiedler, *Love and Death*, p. 450.

35. While of course playing on the voyeuristic fascination this affords the reader. Sedgwick of course develops a similar argument with reference to homosexuality's function as the gothic's unspoken secret. See E. Sedgwick, *Between Men:: English Literature and Male Homosocial Desire* (New York, Columbia University Press, 1985), pp. 94–5.

36. E. Sedgwick, *The Coherence of Gothic Conventions* (New York, Arno Press, 1980), p. 1.

37. Elizabeth Napier for instance argues that: 'The propriety of employing the term Gothic to describe such works is, in any case, open to question.' E. Napier, *The Failure of the Gothic* (Oxford, Clarendon Press, 1987), p. xiii.

38. Sedgwick, *The Coherence of Gothic Conventions*, pp. 8–9.

39. D. Punter, *The Literature of Terror* (London, Longman, 1980), p. 411.

40. O. Evans, *Carson McCullers: Her Life and Work* (London, Peter Owen, 1965), p.45.

41. See J. Butler, *Gender Trouble: Feminism and the Subversion of Identity* (London, Routledge, 1990).

42. Or rather, in the words of Jan Brown as 'fag'. 'Sex, Lies and Penetration: A Butch Finally "Fesses Up"', in J. Nestle, ed., *The Persistent Desire: a Femme Butch Reader* (Boston, Alyson, 1992), pp. 410–15, p. 410.

43. 'For since first setting eyes on Marvin Macy the hunchback was possessed by an unnatural spirit. Every minute he wanted to be following along behind this jailbird, and he was full of silly schemes to attract his attention to himself. Still Marvin Macy either treated him hatefully or failed to notice him at all' (63).

44. Thomson, *The Grotesque*, p. 59.

45. S. Freud, 'The Uncanny', *The Standard Edition*, vol. XVII, trans. J. Strachey (London, The Hogarth Press, 1917–19), pp. 219–52, p. 345.

46. Freud, 'The Uncanny', p. 345.

47. Freud, 'The Uncanny', p. 340.

DOREEN FOWLER

Carson McCullers's Primal Scenes:
The Ballad of the Sad Café

The signature characteristic of Carson McCullers's fiction is her abiding preoccupation with loneliness. Time and again McCullers has acknowledged this preoccupation, and it has become commonplace among critics to observe that a dread of alienation drives her fiction.[1] I call attention to this obsession to note the convergence of southern writer McCullers's perception that unspeakable isolation is the fundamental human condition and French psychoanalyst Jacques Lacan's theory that identity is predicated on alienation. According to Lacan, we are not alone in the beginning because the child perceives itself as part of the mother's body; but to define itself as an "I" separate from the mother, the child must submit to loss—the loss of the mother's body. All of McCullers's works seem to dramatize the estranged condition that Lacan maintains is prerequisite for human subjectivity. Accordingly, we can superimpose Lacan's theory of identity onto McCullers's narratives of loneliness.[2]

Both Freud and Lacan theorize about the unconscious and ultimately claim that what is buried in the unconscious is a guilty desire for a lost presumptive holistic unity. Further, Freud and Lacan propose that repressed material always returns in disguised forms—in dreams, in slips of the tongue, and in literature.[3] McCullers's *Ballad of the Sad Café* represents, I claim, such a disguised return of buried meanings. *The Ballad* opens with a dream image:

From *Critique* 43, no. 3 (Spring 2002). © 2002 by the Helen Dwight Reid Educational Foundation.

a ghostlike face peers from the window of a boarded-up house, "like the terrible dim faces known in dreams" (3). This image serves as notice that we are entering the terrain of the unconscious, that like a dream image, McCullers's *Ballad* constitutes a disguised message from the unconscious mind. Lacan's reformulation of Freud's theory of the unconscious can help us to decipher this message.

Lacan holds that in the beginning, before the formation of identity, in what he calls the imaginary or preoedipal phase, we experience no loneliness, no lack of any kind. In the mother's womb and in the first few months of the child's life, the mother and child exist as one continuous, complete, unbroken circuit; the child does not exist as a separate subject. For identity and cultural meaning to exist, there must be difference, which is predicated upon exclusion. Specifically, the mother must be excluded and must become the first to be Other. (Many others—for example, ethnic, religious, or racial others—follow.) This act of exclusion, which Lacan calls a symbolic self-castration, is the pivotal moment in the emergence of the human subject. At this critical splitting, a desire for a lost imagined integration is driven underground; and, in the words of Terry Eagleton, this buried guilty desire "just is what is called the unconscious" (165). This repression marks the newly constituted subject's entry into the symbolic order, a register of being that overlays the imaginary and is based in absence. The self, then, is born through a division and comes into being fragmented. This narrative of identity as the consequence of loss offers a way to read McCullers's *Ballad*. In fact, the events of the novella appear repeatedly to stage the disguised return and the subsequent repression of the desire to overcome loss.

A rejection of the feminine, identified with the maternal, characterizes both Lacan's symbolic order and the world of McCullers's *Ballad* before Lymon's arrival. Panthea Broughton was the first to observe that *The Ballad* reflects a culture "in flight from the feminine" (41). Miss Amelia, who denies her femininity, is a case in point. As countless critics have observed, before Lymon's appearance, Miss Amelia is masculine not only in her appearance but also in her behavior. In stark antithesis to the feminine maternal, she is domineering, ruthless, aggressive, and exploitative. Both Broughton and Suzanne Morrow Paulson demonstrate that these are the qualities that this culture admires and aspires to. Paulson, in particular, richly documents that Miss Amelia's town is not only "male-dominated" but is also intent on "the murder of the feminine" (188). Arguably, the androcentrism of Miss Amelia's community reflects our own social order writ large, which Lacan submits is male-centered (or phallocentric) because the symbolic order, the register of language, law, and culture, is based in absence, an absence identified with the maternal body.[4] In the constitutive moment, the child rejects the mother and takes for the object of desire the father as presumed originator of being.[5] In other words, Paulson's characterization of Carson McCullers's fictional world, namely that "[e]veryone wants to be the father and to belong to the gang" (194), is also a disturbingly accurate description of Lacan's symbolic order, the order of cultural exchange: one need only read "father-become-Father" for "father" and "symbolic order" for "gang."

This rigid cultural repression of the feminine is relaxed, however, when Lymon appears, and Miss Amelia takes him in. It is noteworthy that Lymon claims to be related to Miss Amelia through his dead mother who he alleges is the half-sister of Miss Amelia's dead mother. Lymon is associated with the dead mother or, in Lacanian terms, the displaced mother of earliest memories. Perhaps that is why Miss Amelia, who is a "solitary" person and was never known to invite anyone to eat with her "unless she was planning to trick them in some way, or make money out of them" (11), now adopts a nurturing attitude toward Lymon. The narrator explains the peculiar tie that develops between Lymon and Miss Amelia in terms of love and observes that "the beloved is only a stimulus for all the stored up love which has lain quiet within the lover for a long time hither to" (26). What the narrator identifies as "falling in love" is another way of naming a disguised eruption of a long-buried desire. The lover's "stored up love" may represent metaphorically what Lacan calls the repressed, the desire for incorporation that was driven underground at the moment of splitting. What Lymon serves to trigger, then, may be a repressed desire to heal the split subject.

The theories of Nancy Chodorow offer a way to interpret Miss Amelia's attachment to Lymon. Chodorow maintains that all adults "look for a return to this emotional and physical union [experienced with the mother before the entry into language and culture]" and that women seek to reproduce this union by becoming mothers themselves (199). Undeniably, Miss Amelia adopts a maternal role toward the child-like Lymon.[6] She carries Lymon on her back and sits by his bedside until he falls asleep. As for Lymon, the narrator is at pains to point out his child-like qualities: he reaches only to the belt buckle of most men; he sucks on candy instead of snuff; and he has "an instinct which is usually found in small children, an instinct to establish immediate vital contact between himself and all things in the world" (20). Thus the relationship between Miss Amelia and Cousin Lymon appears to attempt to reproduce the presumptive unity and integration experienced in an earlier phase of development—the mirror stage.

The mirror stage is an intermediate phase between the imaginary and the symbolic. There can be no reenactment of existence in the imaginary because in that stage the child exists as "an uncognized, material, somatic existence" (Mellard 12). In the mirror stage, the child begins the work of constructing an "I." In the intermediate mirror stage, subjectivity is based in identification with the mother whereas, in the later symbolic phase, identity is predicated upon alienation. The child begins to locate a self, and this sense of self is bestowed on the child by the mother; that is, the mother is the mirror that gives the child a sense of a unified self.

The image is the language of the unconscious, and in *The Ballad* an image appears to signal covertly the return of mirror-stage fusion. On the evening that the café has its origin, when Miss Amelia first permits her customers to buy and drink whisky in "the warm, bright store" (21), she [...] stood most of the evening in the doorway leading to the kitchen" and "most of the time her eyes were fastened lonesomely on the hunchback" (23). A doorway is a frame and, as a frame, suggests a mirror. Looking out from the doorframe, Miss Amelia sees Lymon on the other side as her mirror image, the identificatory imago of mirror-stage fusion.

Miss Amelia's ambivalent feelings on that evening—according to the narrator, "there was in her expression pain, perplexity and uncertain joy" (23)—can also be interpreted in terms of mirror-phase identification. Although in this intermediate stage, identity is based on identification and the yawning gap of the oedipal phase has not yet opened up, nevertheless, in the mirror phase there is not the complete incorporation of the imaginary: There is a distance between the self and the identificatory imago. That space may explain why Miss Amelia wears, in the narrator's words, "the lonesome look of the lover" (23). What the narrator calls "lonesome" Lacan would identify as a repressed desire for incorporation, which has now surfaced disguised. Such desire would cause the lover, in the narrator's words, to "crave any possible relation with the beloved, even if this experience can cause him only pain" (27). The satisfaction of the desire for incorporation would indeed cause the beloved "pain"; it would efface the difference that constitutes identity. Thus the beloved "fears and hates the lover" (27) with good reason: The lover's desire for assimilation threatens the beloved's sense of identity.

A Lacanian framework also provides a fresh way to read the meaning of the café that comes into being as a result of Miss Amelia's relationship with Cousin Lymon. The café is a manifestation of this momentary relaxation of repression. During its brief existence, the people of Miss Amelia's town converge. The café becomes the "warm bright center point of the town" (54); that is, it is a symbol of unity, community, and integration as opposed to the fragmentation that characterizes the postoedipal subject. Interestingly, the café is associated with warmth and the color red. Miss Amelia makes red curtains for the windows; "the great iron stove at the back of the room roared, crackled, and turned red" (54). The emphasis on warmth and the color of blood associates the café with the body; and it is the body, particularly a somatic unity with the mother, that is displaced, leaving a void on accession to the symbolic plane. The café of McCullers's title, then, is the site of a return of a buried desire for a time before alienation and division.[7]

At this juncture, the narrative itself enacts a return in the form of a flashback that the narrator describes as "a curious episode" from "long ago" (27). We are told that Marvin Macy fell in love with Miss Amelia, and they married. I read Marvin Macy's love for Miss Amelia, like Miss Amelia's for Cousin Lymon, as a disguised emergence of a desire that was repressed at the constitution of subjectivity. Once again, Chodorow's theory can be usefully invoked. According to Chodorow, men seek to reenact the "emotional and physical union" that characterized the mother–child relationship in the preoedipal phase by taking wives as substitutes for the rejected mother (199). Applying that thesis to this episode, we can say that Marvin marries Miss Amelia in an attempt to replace the banished mother of the imaginary plane.

Their ten-day marriage, I suggest, is an attempt to reenact mirror-stage identification. Here, also is an image in the text that signifies a return to the mirror phase of development. According to the narrator, Marvin delays "declaring himself" to Miss Amelia for two years. During those years, while he improved himself, "[h]e would stand near the door of her premises his cap in his hand, his eyes meek and longing and misty gray" (29). Standing framed in the door, Marvin sees Amelia on the other side as if she were his mirror image; and he longs for greater intimacy, for total immersion.

This craving for assimilation surfaces on Miss Amelia and Marvin's disastrous wedding night. In psychoanalytic terms, Marvin longs for the incorporation of the imaginary phase and seeks it in the marriage bed. Marvin Macy, the lover, urgently desires what Miss Amelia, the beloved, dreads—the obliteration of distinctions that sexual coupling figures. Thus the unsuccessful outcome of their wedding night is a foregone conclusion.

At another level, Marvin's failure to bring his beloved bride to bed constitutes an abortive primal scene and prefigures the climactic primal scene that is played out at the novella's conclusion. A primal scene, Freud explains, is a child's buried memory of having witnessed parental intercourse. In his later writing, Freud acknowledges that the child may not be remembering an actual witnessed event but may be experiencing a dream or fantasy memory, that is, an archetypal image out of the unconscious mind. This image reflects the child's oedipal desires and his or her related castration anxiety. In the primal tableau, the child observes the father fulfilling the child's desire both to possess and to master the powerful mother. As the child interprets the image of parental intercourse, the father seems to be both satisfying his desire for the mother as well as the mother's desire; paradoxically, the father also appears to be hurting the mother, even castrating her, and the child imagines this is why the mother does not have a penis. This observed tableau serves as a threat to the child: The child will likewise be castrated if she or he continues to desire physical union with the mother. Under the threat of castration, the child renounces the mother; and thus this primal image functions in what Freud calls the oedipal crisis and what Lacan later rewrites as a moment of division that constitutes the fragmented self.

Marvin Macy's failure to consummate his marriage to Miss Amelia represents a failed primal scene. It is a scene of unsuccessful sexual intercourse between a married couple, observed by son-figures, "the young boys who watched through the window on that night" (31). In this evocation of the primal scene, the father-figure, Marvin, is wretchedly unable to play the father's role. As the narrator sagely observes, "A groom is in a sorry fix when he is unable to bring his well-beloved bride to bed with him, and the whole town knows it" (31). Before the watching eyes of the young boys, Marvin is unable to satisfy his desire or the mother's desire; equally important, he fails to appear to disempower the mother. Miss Amelia emerges from the marriage bed as powerful as ever; and Marvin appears to be helpless, as helpless as the watching boys to satisfy or subdue the powerful mother. When, before the child-witnesses, Miss Amelia refuses sexual intercourse, "stomp[s] down the stairs in breeches and a khaki jacket" (31), "slam[s] the kitchen door and give[s] it an ugly kick," and, perhaps most tellingly, "ha[s] a smoke with her father's pipe" (31), she assumes the aspect of the child's fantasy of the phallic mother, the powerful mother of the preoedipal phase, before the appearance of the father. The phallic mother is a child's projection; the child imagines that the mother of the preoedipal stage, who appears to be all-powerful and complete, possesses a penis.

The role of the father in the primal scene is related to what Lacan calls the phallus.[8] The phallus is a difficult Lacanian concept largely because of the connotations the word carries in our culture. In Lacanian terminology, the phallus is not the penis; the phallus is a symbol. It symbolizes the critical moment in the development of subjectivity, the moment when the child, in obedience to the Law of the Father, performs the symbolic self-castration that constitutes identity. Given that the primal scene is an image out of the unconscious for this constitutive moment, the phallus signifies the father's role in this tableau, and in this first rendition of the primal scene in *The Ballad*, Marvin Macy fails to represent the phallus. However, both before and after his fall into loving abjection with Miss Amelia, Marvin, who comes between Miss Amelia and Cousin Lymon, is identified in the text with images that align him with the phallic signifier; specifically, he is infamous for having performed acts of mutilation that symbolize castration. The narrator relates that, as a boy, "for years," Marvin "carried about with him the dried and salted ear of a man he had killed in a razor fight" and that he "had chopped off the tails of squirrels in the pinewoods just to please his fancy" (27–28). In my reading, without his conscious knowledge, Marvin "fanc[ies]" cutting off body-parts of squirrels and people because such acts of mutilation symbolize the severing that constituted identity; they symbolize the always mythical power of the phallus.[9]

Miss Amelia cannot fathom Cousin Lymon's obsession with Marvin Macy, but if we read Marvin in terms of phallic signification, Lymon, who is reenacting with Miss Amelia mirror-stage fusion, desires a representative of the phallic Other, the Other who intervenes in the dyadic relation and ordains subjectivity and loss. "Man's desire," Lacan writes, "is the desire of the Other" (*Écrits* 289). By this, Lacan means that we look to accede to the place of the Other, the place of the constitution of the self, the privileged signifier that appears to hold all signifieds in thrall but does not.[10] When Lymon attempts to explain his fascination with Marvin Macy to Miss Amelia, she is mystified, but Lymon's words imply that he is drawn to Marvin because of his difference: "'Oh Marvin Macy,' groaned the hunchback, and the sound of the name was enough to upset the rhythm of his sobs so that he hiccuped. 'He has been to Atlanta. [...] He has been to the penitentiary,' said the hunchback, miserable with longing" (53). Macy is from a world outside of the closed unit that Lymon and Miss Amelia form. For Lymon, the penitentiary in Atlanta figures the place of the Other, and he "long[s]" to accede to this place that he mistakenly imagines exists outside of loss.

All of McCullers's *Ballad* has been building inexorably toward one climactic event, the battle between Miss Amelia and Marvin. In the psychoanalytic narrative, there is one moment that matters, the moment when the desire for the mother is repressed and the father takes the mother's place as the object of desire. This crucial development in the construction of the ego appears transformed in McCullers's *Ballad* as the epic battle between Marvin Macy and Miss Amelia, which, in turn, takes the form of the novella's second and final primal scene.

The Ballad's second reenactment of the primal scene[11] inverts the traditional formula. Whereas in the traditional primal scene the child-viewer reads sexual coupling as a violent struggle, in McCullers's version, a violent struggle takes on the appearance of sexual coupling. The fight is evoked in distinctly sexual terms; as one sexual image after another appears, we inevitably recall that Miss Amelia and Marvin are still husband and wife but

have not as yet sexually consummated their marriage. It is as if this fight is
that consummation:

> And now that Miss Amelia and Marvin were locked in a hold
> together the crowd came out of its daze and pressed closer. For a
> while the fighters grappled muscle to muscle, their hipbones
> braced against each other. Backward and forward, from side to
> side, they swayed in this way. (67)

This blurring of sex and struggle, which obtains in both the primal scene and
in McCullers's disguised representation of the primal drama, implies a
disturbing unconscious knowledge that love is aligned with power and sex
with violence. The psychoanalytic narrative of identity offers a way to
interpret this troubling alignment: love and sexual intercourse figure the
dyadic unity experienced with the mother of the imaginary plane, and this
original unity ends in a traumatic, violent sundering that constitutes the
fractured subject.

The climax of the novel is the epic struggle between Miss Amelia and
Marvin; and the climax (in all senses of the word) of the battle is Lymon's
decisive intervention.[12] Just as Miss Amelia seems to have won the battle, just
as she has Marvin pinned and her hands encircle his throat, Lymon "sailed
through the air as though he had grown hawk wings," lands on Miss Amelia's
back, and "clutche[s] at her neck with his clawed little fingers" (68). As a
result, Miss Amelia is defeated. At one level, Lyman's intervention signifies
the moment of primary repression, the moment when the child rejects the
mother. Although the Law of the Father requires this separation, it is not the
father, but the child who disrupts the original dyadic unity. Thus Lymon's act
of betrayal can be read as a disguised image for the child's renunciation of the
mother, a necessary step in the formation of identity. At the same time,
Lymon's mythic soaring flight and hawklike descent invites a complementary
reading. The fight takes the form of a primal scene—a scene that makes
palpably evident the father's terrible power and precipitates the child's
rejection of the mother. In this reenactment of the primal scene, however, as
in the failed primal scene on the wedding night, it appears that the mother-
figure is stronger than the father-figure. Describing the terrible contest
between Miss Amelia and Marvin, the narrator twice avers that Miss Amelia
is "the stronger":

> Now the test had come, and in these moments of terrible effort,
> it was Miss Amelia who was the stronger. Marvin Macy was
> greased and slippery, tricky to grasp, but she was stronger.

Gradually she bent him over backward, and inch by inch she forced him to the floor. It was a terrible thing to watch and their deep hoarse breaths were the only sound in the café. At last she had him down, and straddled; her strong big hands were on his throat. (67)

Once again, Marvin Macy is unable to play the father's part in the primal drama, and at the critical moment, "just as the fight was won" (67) by Miss Amelia, Lymon appears to assume supernatural powers and succeeds where Marvin had failed. In this reprise of the primal scene, Lymon, the watching child-figure, assumes the role of father. He symbolically enacts the father's power both to copulate with the mother and to disempower her. When he sails through the air and "land[s] on the broad strong back of Miss Amelia," he assumes the father's position in the act of anal intercourse;[13] and after this figurative intercourse, Miss Amelia is "beaten" and "lay sprawled on the floor, her arms flung outward and motionless," the picture of total abjection (68).

The battle between Marvin and Miss Amelia, which simulates sexual intercourse, ends in a metaphorical sexual consummation, but it is Lymon who experiences this consummation. Observing the fight, Lymon exhibits signs of sexual arousal: "the excitement had made him break out in a rash, and his pale mouth shivered" (67). At the moment when Lymon seems to assume supernatural powers and springs onto Miss Amelia's back from twelve feet away, he utters a cry "that caused a shrill bright shiver to run down the spine" (67). Lymon's cry is the cry of a man experiencing orgasm or, in Lacanian terms, *jouissance*. *Jouissance* is ultimate sexual enjoyment; in French, *jouissance* literally means orgasm. It is the forbidden satisfaction of the sexual drive that Lacan, following Freud, defines as a drive toward self-completion through the Other. *Jouissance* is the always momentary rapture experienced in attempting to reclaim the missing phallus. Lacan uses the sexual term *jouissance* for this ecstasy because sexual intercourse also enacts our desire to have the phallus. In sexual intercourse, the woman is the fetish object substituting for the missing phallus and allowing the man to conceal his phallic lack (Lee 180). Thus *jouissance*, identified with the mythical phallus, is a momentary feeling of empowerment and completion. Lymon experiences this rapturous sense of fulfillment when he ritually enacts the satisfaction of the child's forbidden desire to accede to the place of power, to take the father's place and restore the phallus that can connect us with the mother. To represent *jouissance*, McCullers imaginatively invokes Lymon's orgiastic cry, his ejaculatory leap, and his coital "land[ing]" on Miss Amelia.

Immediately following this moment of triumph Lymon "disappears"

(68). The narrator seems hard-pressed to account for this disappearance; however, from a psychoanalytic point of view, it is the inevitable consequence of Lymon's forbidden *jouissance*. *Jouissance* marks the moment of violating the law against a narcissistic merging[14] and momentarily overcoming lack; however, because identity is defined by absence, where there is no lack, there is no subject. *Jouissance* marks the dissolution of the separate subject and a return to an imaginary unity that preceded subjectivity. It is, Lacan says, "*de trop*" (*Écrits* 319); it is too much; it is the last gasp of the subject as it dissolves into an imaginary relation with the Other. Accordingly, immediately after exhibiting signs of sexual excitation and ritually reenacting the restoration of the forbidden phallic signifier, Lymon temporarily at least "slip[s] out" of view (68).

The novella ends with Miss Amelia's defeat. To drive home that defeat, following the fight, Marvin and Lymon do "everything ruinous they could think of without actually breaking into the office where Miss Amelia stayed the night" (69). The list of "ruinous" deeds—from taking the curios in Miss Amelia's private cabinet to setting out a poisoned dish of her favorite food—suggests that Marvin and Lymon perform every act they can think of to enact ritually the castration of the mythic phallic mother of the preoedipal stage. And then, the narrator tells us, Lymon and Macy go away, opening up the alienation that characterizes the "I" in the symbolic order.

The conclusion of this love story is written in our cultural memory. There can be only one outcome. Both McCullers's subtext and the psychoanalytic narrative propose that all love is in some way an attempt to reenact the first love, and this mother–child relationship must give way to the Law. The imaginary must give way to the symbolic; the mother must give way to the Father.[15] When a desire for return slips past unconscious censors and is recognized, it must be repressed again. Miss Amelia's terrible defeat at the hands of Lymon and Marvin symbolizes this repression. Also it reenacts the all-important moment, the moment of primary repression when a representative of the sign of difference appears and the mother is excluded. The events of *The Ballad* conform to a primal script. Repeatedly throughout the novella a forbidden desire for a lost presumptive wholeness reasserts itself—and is repressed. When Marvin takes his new bride to bed, when Miss Amelia lives with Lymon and "mothers" him, when Lymon ritually enacts a narcissistic merging with the lost mother—all these acts are disguised formulations of a desire to heal the split subject and to restore the missing part lost long ago in an explosive moment of division, the founding moment. Endlessly this desire is repressed and endlessly it returns because, according to Freud, repression, by its very nature, leads to exactly what repression was meant to prevent, the return of the repressed. The desire to break out of human isolation is doomed; at the same time, that desire will never die. Carson McCullers's fable, *The Ballad of the Sad Café*, is an expression of a forbidden undying desire no longer to be alone.

NOTES

1. In the preface to *The Square Root of Wonderful*, for example, McCullers writes: "My central theme is the theme of spiritual isolation. Certainly I have always felt alone" (viii). Two critics who have articulated McCullers's concern with loneliness particularly eloquently are Harold Bloom and Oliver Evans. In the words of Bloom, a "fear of insulation" is "the enabling power of McCullers's imagination" (2). Evans writes: "What she conceives to be the truth about human nature is a melancholy truth: each man is surrounded by a 'zone of loneliness,' serving a life sentence of solitary confinement" (126).

2. I am not proposing that McCullers was influenced by Lacan. Almost certainly McCullers did not know his work. Jacques Lacan's theories were not widely circulated in the United States until the publication of *Écrits* in 1966, and The *Ballad of the Sad Café* was written in the summer of 1941. But a writer does not need a formal knowledge of a theory for meanings that are interpretable by hat theory to figure in his or her work. Freud frequently reiterated the dictum that poets often "discover" what philosophers and others come to theorize about later.

3. In his famous essay, "Repression" (1915), Freud states that "repression itself [...] produces substitutive formations and symptoms, [...] indications of a return of the repressed." Echoing Freud, Lacan states flatly, "repressed, it reappears" (*Écrits* 311.)

4. Lacan states that "there is woman only as excluded by the nature of things which is the nature of words" (*Feminine Sexuality* 144). Lacanian interpreter Jonathan Scott Lee explains that Lacan means that "woman finds herself systematically excluded from reality as constructed in terms of the androcentric symbolic order" (177). Jacqueline Rose cautions against interpreting Lacan's statement to mean that women are excluded from language. She writes: "Woman is excluded by the nature of words, meaning that the definition poses her as exclusion. Note that this is not the same thing as saying that woman is excluded from the nature of words, a misreading which leads to the recasting of the whole problem in terms of woman's place outside language, the idea that women might have of themselves an entirely different speech" (49).

5. It is noteworthy that this Lacanian paradigm is played out in Miss Amelia's life. Her mother is erased in the text (she is mentioned only once—on Miss Amelia's wedding day, she wears her dead mother's wedding dress) and is replaced by her father, whom, even in death, Miss Amelia appears to revere. Miss Amelia, then, may be read as the child who has renounced the mother and identifies with the phallic father and with the Law that forbids merger.

6. Applying a Freudian perspective, Gilbert and Gubar suggest that Lymon represents "the (false) baby as phallus, whose deformity and fake masculinity represent the deformity and fakery that (as Miss Amelia must learn) are associated with her own self-deluding male impersonation" (150).

7. Before Lymon's appearance, the world of *The Ballad* can be read to reflect an imbalance between the imaginary and the symbolic, that is, a culture in which the order identified with the Law that stands for exclusion is dangerously ascendant. The two orders are dependent on one another, and theorists argue that there needs to be a balance between them. Lacanian interpreters, particularly feminist ones, have labored to show

what Jane Gallop calls "the positive and necessary function" of the imaginary. According to Gallop, "the imaginary embodies, fleshes out the skeletal symbolic" (*Daughter's Seduction* 149). Laplanche calls the imaginary "the vital order" (125). The passage into subjectivity, however, is a passage away from the imaginary and into the symbolic; and the imaginary, identified with the rejected mother–child relation and an original formlessness, is resisted and subordinated as we accede to what Jane Gallop calls "the ethical imperative [...] to disrupt the imaginary to reach the symbolic" (*Reading Lacan* 59).

   8. The phallus stands for the loss that is constitutive of identity, and it is associated with the father-become-Father who ordains this separation. Because this moment of splitting constitutes identity and because the father ordains it, the child associates the phallus with power, the power to constitute the self. But, as Jacqueline Rose points out, "this is the ultimate fantasy" (32). The phallus cannot confer complete identity; the phallus is merely a symbol for the rupture that made identity possible. However, human beings continue to identify the phallus with the power to make good our loss.

   9. Although they do not apply a Lacanian methodology, Gilbert and Gubar seem to imply a similar reading of Marvin's symbolic role in the text. They write that Miss Amelia is "caught between two phallic beings, the one exploitative, the other vengeful" (150).

   10. Lacan defines the Other as the always posited but never grasped original signifier of being. We look to the Other to guarantee meaning, but, in Lacan's words, "there is no Other of the Other" (*Écrits* 311); that is, there is no transcendental or fixed sign that imbues our cultural signifiers with meaning.

   11. Gilbert and Gubar have observed that the struggle between Miss Amelia and Marvin takes the form of a primal scene. They state that "the spectacular fight in which Marvin Macy and Miss Amelia engage before a mass of spectators [...] is the primal scene of sexual consummation which did not take place on their wedding night" (151).

   12. Gilbert and Gubar offer several provocative other interpretations of Lymon's decisive intervention in the struggle. Each of them resonates interestingly with my own. In one Freudian reading, they interpret Miss Amelia as being punished for "penis envy." In another, the fight signals the moment when she is forced to confront her desire for Marvin Macy. In the third, Miss Amelia is the medium for a homosexual bonding between Lymon and Macy. It should perhaps also be explained that Gilbert and Gubar's purpose is to reveal that McCullers has "internalized just the horror at independent womanhood which marks the writings of literary men from Faulkner to Wylie" (147). I would modify that statement and say that McCullers has psychically internalized an exclusionary model of identity and the social order.

   13. Freud uncovers the primal scene in the course of analyzing a patient identified as the Wolf Man, who, as a child, either witnessed his parents engaged in *coitus a tergo* or imagined such a scene after having observed animals copulating. For a full discussion of the primal scene, see Freud's case study of the "Wolf Man," *Standard Edition* 17:36, 77–80, 107–09. See also Brooks, "Fictions of the Wolf Man: Freud and Narrative Understanding" in *Reading for the Plot*.

   14. All attempts to restore the phallus are prohibited by the Law of the Father. In fact, Lacan writes that the Law is the Law against *jouissance*: "But we must insist that *jouissance* is forbidden to him who speaks as such, although it can only be said between the lines for whoever is subject of the Law, since the Law is grounded in this very prohibition" (*Écrits* 319).

   15. In the words of Terry Eagleton, "The presence of the father, symbolized by the phallus, teaches the child that it must take up a place in the family which is defined by sexual difference, by exclusion (it cannot be its parent's lover) and by absence (it must relinquish its earlier bonds to the mother's body)" (167).

WORKS CITED

Bloom, Harold. Introduction. *Carson McCullers*. Ed. Harold Bloom. New York: Chelsea, 1986.

Brooks, Peter. *Reading for the Plot: Design and Intention in Narrative*. New York: Knopf, 1984.

Broughton, Panthea. "Rejection of the Feminine in Carson McCullers's *The Ballad of the Sad Café*." *Twentieth Century Literature* 20 (January 1974): 34–43.

Chodorow, Nancy. *The Reproduction of Mothering: Psychoanalysis and the Sociology of Gender*. Berkeley: U of California P, 1978.

Clark, Beverly Lyon and Melvin J. Friedman, eds. *Critical Essays on Carson McCullers*. New York: Hall, 1996.

Eagleton, Terry. *Literary Theory: An Introduction*. Minneapolis: U Minnesota P, 1983.

Evans, Oliver. "The Case of Carson McCullers." Clark and Friedman 124–28.

Freud, Sigmund. *The Standard Edition of the Complete Psychological Works of Freud*. Ed. and trans. James Strachey. 24 vols. London: Hogarth, 1961.

Gallop, Jane. *The Daughter's Seduction: Feminism and Psychoanalysis*. Ithaca: Cornell UP, 1982.

———. *Reading Lacan*. Ithaca: Cornell UP, 1985.

Gilbert, Sandra M. and Susan Gubar. "Fighting for Life." Clark and Friedman 147–54.

Lacan, Jacques. *Écrits: A Selection*. Trans. by Alan Sheridan. 1966. New York: Norton, 1977.

Laplanche, Jean. *Life and Death in Psychoanalysis*. Trans. by Jeffrey Mehlman. Baltimore: Johns Hopkins UP, 1976.

Lee, Jonathan Scott. *Jacques Lacan*. Amherst: U of Massachusetts P, 1990.

McCullers, Carson. *The Ballad of the Sad Café and Other Stories*. New York: Bantam, 1971.

———. Preface. *The Square Root of Wonderful: A Play*. Boston: Houghton, 1971.

Mellard, James M. *Using Lacan, Reading Fiction*. Urbana: U of Illinois P, 1991.

Mitchell, Juliet, ed. *Feminine Sexuality: Jacques Lacan and the "Ecole Freudienne."* Ed. and trans. Jacqueline Rose. New York: Norton, 1992.

Paulson, Suzanne Morrow. "Carson McCullers's *The Ballad of the Sad Café*: A Song Half Sung, Misogyny, and 'Ganging Up.'" Clark and Friedman 187–205.

Rose, Jacqueline. Introduction. Mitchell 27–57.

SARAH GLEESON-WHITE

Two Bodies in One:
The Heart Is a Lonely Hunter *and*
The Ballad of the Sad Café

Fundamental to this account of the grotesque in McCullers's texts is the anxiety attending the formation of identity. This anxiety takes the form of various tensions, which include those between the adolescent promise of lines of flight and social demands for conformity, between the male body and its feminization, and between femininity and masculinity. The Bakhtinian concept of "two bodies in one" (*Rabelais* 52) can elucidate what is occurring in such tensions.

Most immediately, "two bodies in one" conjures up the figure of androgyny. Although there are several characters whom we might consider androgynous, such as Singer, Mick, and Frankie, I will focus on a comparison between male androgyny, in the figure of Biff Brannon, and female androgyny, in the figure of Miss Amelia Evans, in terms of classical androgyny and what I term "grotesque androgyny" to reveal that androgyny predicated on classical notions of synthesis and wholeness cannot adequately account for the types of subjectivity McCullers's texts explore. Traditional concepts of androgyny rely on the assumption that masculinity and femininity have a fixed essence, whereas, as we have seen, McCullers conceives of gender in terms of masquerade. Not only is gender nomadic, but it is the tension *between* gendered subject possibilities that produces McCullers's grotesque subjects.

From *Strange Bodies: Gender and Identity in the Novels of Carson McCullers*. © 2003 by the University of Alabama Press.

First, then, I trace more traditional readings of androgyny in both *The Heart Is a Lonely Hunter* and *The Ballad of the Sad Café*, highlighting their limitations. I then weigh up the efficacy or otherwise of the Bakhtinian model of "two bodies in one." This involves a close examination of the concept of hybridity and different accounts of it in relation to McCullers's texts, as well as the idea of "spanning" as set out in her poem "Father, Upon Thy Image We Are Spanned," with the aim of recovering the meaning of grotesque subjectivity in McCullers's writings as a whole.

CLASSICAL ANDROGYNY

Classical conceptions of androgyny derive from Aristophanes' account, in Plato's *Symposium* (59–61, 190b–191c), of an early people whom he calls hermaphroditic. Aristophanes's hermaphrodite is representative of the ideal state of man. This symmetrical figure was one of three sexes[1] and had "the characteristics of both male and female," "with two organs of generation." All three sexes independently formed "a rounded whole ... complete circle," an aesthetic of unity also found in the ephebic statuary of classical antiquity. To curb the power of these "formidable" figures, Zeus decided "to cut each of them in two." Platonic androgyny, then, represents a utopia of genderless innocence, before the fall into male and female, masculine and feminine.

Platonic formulations of androgyny persist in twentieth-century psychoanalytical discourse. Freud makes use of Plato's myth in "The Sexual Aberrations" to reflect the role of the sexual instinct according to which human beings "are always striving to unite again in love" (46).[2] Twentieth-century writers influenced by Platonic notions include Woolf, who explores the "great" androgynous mind in *A Room of One's Own*.[3] The sight of a young man and woman climbing into a taxi prompts her to think of the "unity of the mind": "The normal and comfortable state of being is that when the two love in harmony together, spiritually cooperating. If one is a man, still the woman part of the brain must have effect; and a woman also must have intercourse with the man in her.... It is when fusion takes place that the mind is fully fertilized and uses all its faculties" (92).

In the latter part of the century, the classical/psychoanalytical conception of androgyny inflects Anglo-American feminism of the 1960s and 1970s, of which June Singer and Carolyn Heilbrun are particularly representative. Both draw on Jungian concepts of the feminine and the masculine to call for a "recognition" of the androgynous mind, which would provide the potential to liberate both men and women from an either/or pattern of "appropriate behavior" (see Singer; Heilbrun, *Toward a Recognition*). The concept drew much criticism in the 1980s for its indifference to specific female concerns.[4] Nearly a decade after the publication of *Toward a Recognition of Androgyny*, Heilbrun continued to refute criticism by claiming that androgyny "seeks to suggest that sex roles are societal constructs which ought to be abandoned." Although she does admit that androgyny is only "a necessary stopping place on the road to feminism" ("Androgyny" 265), her concept (and defense) of androgyny neglects two differently marked bodies.

Several readings of androgyny in McCullers's novels emerged in the 1980s. Writing in much the same vein as Singer and Heilbrun, these commentators view androgyny as a positive and productive concept of "wholeness." For example, the supposed androgyny of Biff Brannon in *The Heart Is a Lonely Hunter* is equated with "artistic awareness" (Taetzsch 192), and it seems that "only the androgyns are capable of attempting to escape the isolation of man" (Box 117). Significantly, when it comes to the question of Miss Amelia's androgyny, she is identified as "grotesque, freak, queer.... witch-wizzard [*sic*]" (Carlton 60), or as "hermaphroditic" (Kahane, "Gothic Mirror" 347), which is the "bad" reality of the androgynous ideal, for the hermaphrodite is a freak (Garber, *Vice Versa* 211, 214, 218). In the following comparative examination of Amelia and Biff, which focuses on the trope of pregnancy as it is evoked by androgyny, I reveal the dissymmetry[5] of such a universal ideal. That is to say, the androgynous woman and the androgynous man mean quite differently. To ignore this difference is to ignore the nomadism and tension of subjectivity in McCullers's writings.

Due to the discrepant identification of Amelia and Biff as androgynes in critical writings, we must first establish that both characters can in fact be designated androgynous if the same criteria are applied. Since Biff's femininity and Amelia's masculinity have been discussed at great length in previous chapters, it is sufficient merely to note here Biff's masculine traits and Amelia's feminine traits in order to establish their respective androgyny.

While Biff looks masculine—his body is hard and hairy—he also has a stereotypically rational masculine mind. In the outline of *The Heart Is a Lonely Hunter*, McCullers describes Biff as "nearly always coldly reflective.... He has a passion for detail. It is typical of him that he has a small room ... devoted to a complete and neatly catalogued file of the daily evening newspaper dating back without a break for eighteen years" ("Author's Outline" 146).[6] Throughout the text of the novel itself are many references to Biff as a thinker (*H* 17, 111–12, 116, 118, 120, 190, 302). At times Biff seems obsessive, for example, in his almost fetishistic cataloging of the newspapers. At other times he reveals uncanny insight, as when he perceives Singer's function as a personal god for the four "friends." Biff wonders:

"[W]hy did everyone persist in thinking the mute was exactly as they wanted him to be—when most likely it was all a very queer mistake?" (*H* 197).

Strongly opposed to this type of masculine mind is the feminine intuitive mind, represented by Miss Amelia's superstitious beliefs, for example, in numerology. Furthermore, although she refuses to treat "female complaints," Amelia is nonetheless a powerful healer and "there was no disease so terrible but she would undertake to cure it" (*H* 23). And, to note again, it could be argued that Miss Amelia's love for Lymon also "feminizes" her. So, Amelia does manifest feminine traits. Somehow, in the critical literature, Amelia's rejection of heterosexuality has become indicative of her flight from the feminine. According to this rather suspect logic, we could also charge Biff, who refuses the "male role," with "flight from the masculine," thus barring him from "true" androgynous status. Nevertheless, for the sake of argument, Biff Brannon is as androgynous as Miss Amelia. Both show traits of the "other" gender as well as their "own" respective gender in both their appearance and behavior. However, to reiterate, curiously enough, very rarely in the critical literature is Amelia referred to as "androgynous."[7] In the main, such a label is reserved for Biff Brannon.

There is one further trait Miss Amelia and Biff Brannon share: a strong maternal/paternal desire, which paradoxically eschews physical reproduction. The image of pregnancy is a fantasy evoked by the figure of androgyny. According to psychoanalytic theory, androgyny is equated "with a repressed desire to return to the imaginary wholeness and self-sufficiency associated with the pre-Oedipal phase before sexual difference" (Weil 3). That is to say, the fantasy of motherhood/fatherhood conjures up the image of a pre-Oedipal plenitude, which is associated with classical androgyny and involves the erasure of lapsarian sexual difference as, for instance, in Aristophanes's hermaphrodite. To focus on the trope of pregnancy in *The Heart Is a Lonely Hunter* and *The Ballad of the Sad Café* is to draw out once and for all the inherent dissymmetry or sexual indifference of classical androgynous wholeness.

Biff is "both maternal and paternal" (Phillips, "Gothic Architecture" 65): he sends whiskey to Doctor Copeland's son, Willie, while he is in prison; he treats his niece, Baby Wilson, as one of his own; he offers Jake Blount only kindness, both material and otherwise. Furthermore, Biff yearns to be both omnipotent mother and father at once, that is, to give birth without procreative sexuality. There is a part of Biff "that sometimes almost wished he was a mother and that Mick and Baby were his kids" (*H* 119). Lucile remarks that "'you'd make a good mother.' 'Thanks,' Biff said. 'That's a compliment'" (*H* 203). Not surprisingly, he yearns "[t]o adopt a couple of little children. A boy and a girl. About three or four years old so they would always feel like he was their own father. Their Dad. Our Father.... In the summer the three of them would go to a cottage on the Gulf.... And then they would bloom as he grew old. Our Father" (*H* 207). One reader concludes that Biff's "androgyny does not stand opposed either to women or to procreation." Instead, Biff will combine the two: "Biff dreams of nurturing, self-sacrificing, interactive responsibilities, not of fathering as opposed to mothering, but of parenting. Nor is parenting necessarily biological" (Budick 159). According to this view, Biff is the "pregnant man," equated with androgynous plenitude, for "the common representation of the hermaphrodite is that of a figure endowed with breasts and a penis; the female genitalia do not figure.... Seen in this light, the hermaphrodite appears less as a woman with a penis and more as a man with breasts." Significantly, the androgynous fantasy of the pregnant man allows the male access to "the powerful status he himself attributed to his mother" (Pacteau 74, 76). This scene is played out in *The Heart Is a Lonely Hunter* in Biff's relationship to his own mother, of whom he is in great awe: "She was a tall, strong woman with a sense of duty like a man. She had loved him best. Even now he sometimes dreamed of her. And her worn gold wedding ring stayed on his finger always" (199).

Similarly, Amelia has maternal yearnings that do not involve physical procreation. The text constructs her as "the phallic woman" of psychoanalytic theory, the female equivalent (which, I will argue, is in no way equivalent) of the pregnant man. Like the pregnant man, the phallic woman suggests a pre-Oedipal plenitude, representing "the child's fantasy of an omnipotent and absolutely powerful, sexually neutral figure" (Grosz, "Phallic Mother" 314). Just as Biff's relationship with his mother might explain his androgyny, so might Amelia's with her father. In *The Ballad of the Sad Café*, Amelia is raised alone by her father (20) who, after his death, "was ... an interminable subject which was dear to her.... Miss Amelia never mentioned her father to anyone else except Cousin Lymon. That was one of the ways in which she showed her love for him" (45–46). Thus, her androgyny could stem from a desire to incorporate the power of the father, the phallus.

With no children of her own, Amazonian and sexually uninterested, Amelia, in her role of healer, behaves as a mother toward the sick children: she makes up special "gentler and sweeter" potions so that they might avoid the often violent effects of the powerful adult drugs (*B* 22). Mother-like, Amelia responds compassionately to Lymon's tears when he first arrives in town (*B* 14), and as her love develops, she comes to watch over him protectively: "There was a softness about her grey, queer eyes and she was smiling gently to herself. Occasionally she glanced from the hunchback to the other people in the café—and then her look was proud, and there was in it the hint of a threat, as though daring anyone to try to hold him to account for all his foolery" (*B* 50). "She spoiled him to a point beyond reason" (*B* 31), putting him to bed in the evenings, making sure that his prayers have been said before tucking him in (*B* 54). Lymon is for Amelia "a child acquired without pain" (Millichap, "Carson McCullers" 335), just as Mick Kelly and Baby Wilson are for Biff Brannon. It is fair to conclude, as the townsfolk do, that if Amelia and Lymon "had found some satisfaction between themselves, then it was a matter concerning them and God alone. All sensible people agreed in their opinion about this conjecture—and their answer was a plain, flat no" (*B* 33–33).

Biff's refrain, "Our Father" (*H* 207), cited earlier, epitomizes the pre-Oedipal plenitude already suggested by the maternal/paternal yearnings of the androgynous Amelia and Biff. He is the pregnant man, while she is the phallic woman. However, there is an obvious dissymmetry between the man and the woman who seek androgyny. Psychoanalytic theory, for example, does not consider (the fantasy of) the androgynous pregnant man a menacing figure. At worst, he represents "a descent into feminine castration and abjection." On the other hand, the fantasy of the phallic *woman*, in her "monstrous ascent into phallicism," is a powerful and unsettling figure in psychoanalytic discourse: "[H]aving the phallus is much more destructive as a feminine operation than as a masculine one, a claim that ... implies that there is no other way for women to assume the phallus except in its most killing modalities" (Butler, *Bodies That Matter* 103).

Within the framework of the menacing fantasy of the phallic woman, it could be said that the phallic/uncastrated/masculine Miss Amelia becomes the castrator of Marvin Macy: she denies him the position of having the phallus in order to save her own phallic position. This bears out Butler's assertion that "[t]he failure to submit to castration appears capable of producing only its opposite, the spectral figure of the castrator.... The figure of excessive phallicism, typified by the phallic mother, is devouring and destructive, the negative fate of the phallus when attached to the feminine position" (*Bodies That Matter* 102). Amelia must therefore be punished as, in fact, she is.

As I noted in the preceding chapter, Amelia's more threatening status as the Amazonian phallic woman may lie in the fact that her masculinity, or androgyny, is manifested publicly, while Biff's androgyny occurs in private. Nevertheless, as readers, we of course have access to Biff's private feminine performance and yearnings, and it is in the responses of various McCullers commentators that the shortcomings of androgyny, in terms of its *indifference*, can be found.

In "The Flowering Dream," McCullers describes Amelia's maternal love for the hunchback dwarf as "strange" (287). Within *The Ballad of the Sad Café* itself, Amelia's rejection of sexual relations in favor of an asexual maternal love is viewed as an oddity. For example, when earlier Amelia weds Marvin Macy, the townsfolk, who had hoped that it would turn her into "a calculable woman," consider the fiasco of the unconsummated marriage "unholy" (38). The crucial element here is the condemnation heaped on Miss Amelia for her refusal to gather bride-fat, as well as for her later asexual, and so nonreproductive, relationship with a dwarf. The responses of the text's readers reflect such condemnation: Amelia is chastised for kicking out Marvin Macy (a mere "mischief-maker") and blamed for his subsequent life of crime (Roberts 94–95); Marvin Macy is, remember, no less than a rapist; or Amelia is censured for her rejection of heterosexuality.[8] These critics implicitly equate women's function with heterosexual reproduction. Amelia is therefore condemned, both inside and outside the ballad, for her rejection of "womanly" procreative duties, underscored by her "strange" maternal, nonsexual love for Cousin Lymon.

Conversely, Lucile (along with several commentators) deems it acceptable for Biff Brannon to indulge his maternal/paternal predilection toward both Mick Kelly and Baby Wilson, and to adopt children. Although Biff himself senses something "wrong" (*H* 25) in his unusual feelings, his odd desires are nevertheless left unchallenged while Amelia's are not.[9] There is no doubt, however, that Biff's feelings toward Mick are not merely those of a caring parent. There are definite sexual nuances in Biff's relationship with the young tomboy.[10] Barely able to speak to Mick (*H* 20, 109, 199), Biff blushes at the mere sight of her (*H* 186). On another occasion, "He watched her as she stood behind the counter and he was troubled and sad. He wanted to reach out his hand and touch her sunburned, tousled hair—but not as he had ever touched a woman" (*H* 109).

L. Taetzsch asserts, rather cryptically, that Biff's feeling for Mick is "not the sexuality of a man toward a woman, but an androgyn toward an androgyn" (194). Certainly, Biff acknowledges that he would like to touch Mick as he never has a woman, but this in no way discounts other forms of pleasure and desire. (In any case, Taetzsch's argument could just as easily apply to Miss Amelia's affection for the seemingly sexless Cousin Lymon.) Biff censures himself to some extent for his strange desire for Mick: four weekends in a row, Biff "had walked in the neighborhood where he might see Mick. And there was something about it that was—not quite right. Yes. Wrong" (*H* 205). Biff's feeling of "tenderness" for Mick makes him "uneasy" (*H* 23, 109). "He had done nothing wrong but in him he felt a strange guilt. Why? The dark guilt of all men, unreckoned and without a name" (*H* 205).

Perhaps this dark guilt refers to a fascination with the sexually undifferentiated prepubescent body. This would make sense of the fact that once Mick grows into womanhood, Biff feels "only a sort of gentleness. In him the old feeling was gone. For a year this love had blossomed strangely. He had questioned it a hundred times and found no answer" (*H* 311).

Furthermore, while rejection of heterosexual desire is a negative trait in Amelia, curiously, Biff's asexuality seems to be a mark of superior character. Budick, for example, hails "Biff's denial of his sexuality" as a sign that he is "not limited by biology." She goes on: "Biff will adopt ... children, not produce them biologically.... Biff is not restricted by convention" (151, 159). For some reason, however, Miss Amelia is heavily delimited by cultural attitudes and constrictions. Her shunning of reproductive sexuality means only that she is a reprehensible, mannish freak.

In fact, Biff's impotence becomes a sign of the transcendence of the *drech*—the "intake and alimentation and reproduction" (*H* 204)—of human experience, to fulfill the dream of androgynous wholeness. Biff's impotence supposedly allows him to "embrace ... a metamorphosis into a more enlightened entity," "into artistic, enlightened androgyny" (Taetzsch 192–93).[11] Thus, while Amelia is entwined in the equation woman/mother, Biff, the man, can transcend the body to be the androgynous Everyman, the universal transcendent subject, freed from the bodily constraints of sex. That Biff is impotent and thus genitally "distanced" only furthers these contrasting constructions of "man" and "woman": he can be representative of the "human," while Amelia, on the other hand, is caught in the boarded-up building, her body.

It is generally agreed that Alice Brannon, Biff's wife, plays an important role in his "developing androgyny." For example, along with his impotence, Alice's death enables Biff "to effect within himself a kind of marriage between the male and female, and his direct sexual needs are sublimated into parental emotions" (Roberts 83).[12] In some sense, Alice is killed off in the text so that Biff's developing androgyny can manifest itself. What is suggested here is male appropriation of the feminine, a problem that has great currency today when many male Continental philosophers espouse a kind of "becoming-woman" or a "feminine voice." We must ask in response, how does this affect real women? Reconsidered in this light, Biff's private (and for the most part unremarked-upon) appropriation of Alice's femininity subtly insinuates that he can perform femininity better than she ever could. Alice, the "real" woman, seems to be superfluous. So, Biff Brannon is not a fine model for the "recognition of androgyny" but, conceivably, the usurper of Alice's feminine subjectivity, of her experience as a woman. This clearly counters the claim, mentioned earlier, that "Biff's androgyny does not stand opposed ... to women" (Budick 159).

Biff believes that Alice makes him "tough and small and as common as she was" (*H* 17). To lessen her defiling affects, the couple call each other "Mister and Misses [*sic*]" (*H* 17), they do not sleep together (*H* 32), and he will not undress in front of her (*H* 32). In sum, Biff is repulsed by "his good-looking plump wife" (*H* 56). It is Alice who apparently impedes Biff's developing androgyny and who has "forced" him "to superficially assume the male role.... After her death he takes a complete bath [*H* 112], an action which suggests his washing himself of the male role as well as his recognizing that he no longer needs to be physically repugnant. He then becomes more androgynous, feeling no necessity to hide his sensitivity by conforming to a static sex role" (Box 122).[13] Again, it is as if Biff can transcend the *drech* of human being. Oddly, in this reading, it is *masculinity* that appears to be the muddying gender, something of which Biff needs to be cleansed before he can assume Alice's femininity. More commonly, it is femininity, the female body, that is aligned with the abject.

Because Alice impedes Biff's androgyny, she must be annulled. The text therefore kills her off, for it is what she *represents*, that is, femininity, that is of real significance for the man seeking androgyny. And once she dies, Biff cannot remember anything about her, except for "her feet—stumpy, very soft and white and with puffy little toes" (*H* 117).[14] In a similar way, Biff feels that the only way to deal with Alice when she is alive is with silence (*H* 17). He has, in a sense, usurped her and colonized the very memory of her. Thus, within the dynamic of appropriation, it is absence that marks "real" women, and what is emphasized is the death of the other; in this case, it is a literal death.

The Heart Is a Lonely Hunter constructs Alice's femininity quite differently from the femininity Biff later appropriates. While Alice is alive, Biff considers her a petty nagger (120). Yet once Biff takes on Alice's apparently annoying idiosyncrasies, he transforms them into an androgynous ideal. According to the logic of appropriation, it makes sense, then, that it is *after* Alice's death that Biff begins to yearn to adopt children (207). By improving on Alice's own feminine traits, rendered stereotypical in her, Biff is able to incorporate them into his (male) self to become the omnipotent maternal/paternal "Our Father." Biff ponders this dynamic himself when, buffing his nails as Alice buffed hers (56) and using her Agua Florida and lemon hair rinse, he wonders: "Certain whims that he had ridiculed in Alice were now his own. Why?" (198). And again: "[T]he one who has gone is not really dead, but grows and is created for a second time in the soul of the living" (111).[15] This analysis makes apparent a rather sinister implication of male androgyny: through Biff's appropriation of Alice's seemingly second-rate femininity, he is better able to control and then to rearticulate the feminine according to his own (male) terms, separating the feminine from the experience of "real" female subjectivity at the same time. By denigrating Alice's womanliness and subsequently appropriating it, Biff makes Alice the ground to his figure, to his androgynous self-representation.

In his appropriation of the feminine, Biff Brannon is reminiscent of Ovid's Tiresias, who is empowered by his foray into femininity to return a better man (67). Biff Brannon, too, becomes a seer as he accesses, even if briefly, "a glimpse of human struggle and of valour," as one eye "delved narrowly into the past" and the other "gazed wide and affrighted into a future of blackness, error, and ruin" (*H* 312). While we might associate the androgynous Biff with the seer, a shaman-like figure,[16] significantly, when it comes to the question of Miss Amelia's legendary powers, she is labeled a witch.[17] Unlike Biff, she is never accorded shamanistic status. Furthermore, again like Tiresias, Biff returns a man—"But, motherogod, was he a sensible than or not?" (*H* 312). Biff's story is "the safe story of the recovery of reason" (Spivak, "Three Feminist Readings" 24).

I have shown that the concept of classical androgyny is primarily a male aspiration and a male achievement. It is also potentially a misogynistic image: first, in its denial of any true androgyny for the woman who becomes instead a dangerous freak, unrepresentative of the Platonic ideal, and second, insofar as the male subject colonizes femininity, which he then performs in a superior fashion. I would agree with the assertion, then, that androgyny "rests on the assumption that the kind of body we have puts no limits on the personalities we might develop; this is really just like Plato's assumption that any kind of soul or mind can exist in our bodies" (Spelman 124). A static model such as classical androgyny ignores the many tensions in McCullers's fictional worlds.

GROTESQUE ANDROGYNY

Given the inadequacy of the classical model, the type of androgyny Bakhtin describes in *Rabelais and His World* is a more useful model with which to illuminate the irresolvable tensions of identity in McCullers's texts. Although also concerned with the notion of "two in one," grotesque androgyny is open-ended and always in process, not a completed whole. No synthesis takes place; the "two in one" is, literally, the image of the unfinished.

Like the classical model, however, Bakhtin's configuration of grotesque androgyny seems to appropriate the feminine. Bakhtin's "two bodies in one" does not merely invoke the fantasy of pregnancy as classical androgyny does; it explicitly uses images of the pregnant body as its basis. To recall, the grotesque rests on the image of the pregnant body. Bearing in mind that the

Bakhtinian carnival world is open to men alone (*Rabelais* 13), the image of the pregnant "two bodies in one" recalls the "pregnant man" of androgynous plenitude. Thus, as with the classical model of androgyny, women once more risk becoming the ground for male carnivalesque subjectivity.

Bakhtin's focus on the "material bodily lower stratum," which gives birth to carnivalesque subjectivity, invokes the image of the pregnant body time and time again: "This is the pregnant and begetting body, or at least a body ready for conception and fertilization, the stress being laid on the phallus or the genital organs. From one body a new body always emerges in some form or other" (*Rabelais* 26).[18] Intertwined with such images of birth and pregnancy are those of death, for death is part of the process of renewal: "To degrade is to bury, to sow, and to kill simultaneously, in order to bring forth something *more and better*. To degrade also means to concern oneself with the lower stratum of the body.... Degradation digs a bodily grave for a new birth; it has not only a destructive, negative aspect, but also a regenerating one" (*Rabelais* 21, emphasis added).[19] This suggests once more the death, or at least the absence, of the other, which leads to the birth of the new subject. Just as Biff emerges a "more and better" person after Alice's death, as he appropriates her feminine vitality, the new body of which Bakhtin conceives, also born from death, is a "more and better" body. In a dynamic congruent to the relationship between Alice and Biff, the grotesque body, with its conjoined images of birth and death, enacts a "caesarian operation [which] kills the mother but delivers the child" (*Rabelais* 106). This image recalls Alice's death from "a tumour almost the size of a newborn child" in *The Heart Is a Lonely Hunter* (110).[20]

It can be argued, then, that misuse or appropriation of the feminine for the creation of a new identity occurs throughout *Rabelais and His World*. For example, woman is "first of all ... the *principle* that gives birth. She is the womb" (200, emphasis added).[21] As mentioned, it is the male subject, the new man, to which she gives birth. In *The Ballad of the Sad Café*, for example, the androgynous Amelia is defeated in giving birth to a new form of subjectivity for herself. Like Alice, she is killed off, made absent, to allow for the birth of the alliance between Marvin Macy and Cousin Lymon. Thus, once more, woman's experience becomes superfluous as the *idea* of the feminine is rent from her reality. It is frequently argued that at the same time that women are excluded from carnivalesque subjectivity, they are also "the *other* that enables the perspective of the free and open-ended (male) *I*" (Ginsburg 167). These charges are reminiscent of those made against classical androgyny.

There is another element of Bakhtin's delineation of androgyny that several feminist commentators find problematic. This is that the maternal, the female, and the grotesque become equated with one another (Ginsburg 166, 170).[22] In *Rabelais and His World*, there is no alternative model of feminine subjectivity to the maternal grotesque. So, woman is caught within the strictures of reproductive functions. There are, however, several ways in which McCullers's texts engage with the problems resulting from Bakhtin's grave/womb image, that is, the problems of male appropriation of the feminine and of the alignment of the female with the grotesque and maternal body.

To re-address the issue of feminine appropriation in *The Heart Is a Lonely Hunter*, it is worthwhile to look closely at the effects that a newly acquired femininity has on Biff Brannon. Counter to what many believe, namely, that he is enriched and enlightened by his androgyny, Biff's femininity is, rather, symbolic of his decline. In a sense, it is as if femininity avenges itself. The feminine here is not "pregnant" but disempowering and debilitating. I have repeatedly cited the subversive influence of femininity or the feminine in McCullers's fiction: as the unruly and spectacular body of the adolescent girls; as an unmanning force on the ideal male body; and as a parodic dynamic in the hyperbolically feminine women. Although the lack of adult women and their voices constitutes a major gap in McCullers's texts, when the feminine comes to work on different bodies, it becomes a powerful force. The femininity Biff acquires from Alice is no exception.

By mapping onto Biff's androgyny this conceptualization of femininity and woman as it occurs in McCullers's texts, we quickly realize that Biff's increasing androgyny actually signals his impotence as he performs "like a woman," that is, as a castrated man. After Alice's death, Biff begins to feel old, although he is only forty-four (*H* 205, 209), and "the business was losing money. There were many slack hours" (*H* 199). Caught up in a crippling nostalgia (*H* 120, 199, 208), "uneasy" and "afraid" (*H* 311), he is left with no one person to love, "leaving him either better or worse. Which? However you looked at it" (*H* 310). McCullers herself discusses the association of Biff's enervation with his femininity in her "Author's Outline of 'The Mute'": "at forty-four years [Biff] is prematurely impotent," and "as a compensation for his own dilemma," he believes that "human beings are fundamentally ambisexual—and for confirmation he turns to the periods of childhood and senility" (146). McCullers adds that Biff's acquisition of his dead wife's habits is "a reflection of his own feeling for his approaching decline and death" (148).

In *The Heart Is a Lonely Hunter*, Biff concludes that "by nature all people are of both sexes.... The proof? Because old men's voices grow high and reedy and they take on a mincing walk. And old women sometimes grow fat and their voices get rough and deep and they grow dark little moustaches.

And he even proved it himself—the part of him that sometimes almost wished he was a mother" (119). Thus, his growing femininity is contiguous with the unmanning effects of old age and impotence. That this is the case undermines the many accounts that point to Biff's dream of wholeness, that is, the androgynous ideal. At the very end of *The Heart Is a Lonely Hunter*, Biff rejects his status as the "androgynous" seer to became once more a "sensible man."

The dynamic in androgyny, of a femininity that castrates the male, is also apparent in Ovid's story of Hermaphroditus in *Metamorphoses*. Seduced by the nymph, Salmacis, Hermaphroditus becomes two bodies in one: he "saw that the water had made him half a man, / With limbs all softness ... a voice whose tone was almost treble" (93). Unlike the hermaphrodite of *Symposium*, in Ovid's story there is no sense of completion and wholeness. Hermaphroditus is indicative of the fallen state of man who is "contaminated" by female desire/Salmacis, not the utopian model Aristophanes' hermaphrodite signifies. Femininity in *The Heart Is a Lonely Hunter* has a similar overpowering force.

It is not just the male androgyny whose debility coincides with femininity. Amelia Evans, at the end of her story, is defeated by the conventions of a society that demands she become the personification of the principle of woman. As Westling notes, after Amelia's defeat in the fight, "it is the unmistakable body of a woman we see lying on the floor of the café" (177). Amelia "lay sprawled on the floor, arms flung outwards and motionless.... Someone poured water on Miss Amelia, and after a time she got up slowly and dragged herself into her office ... she was sobbing with the last of her grating, winded breath.... Once she gathered her right fist together and knocked it three times on the top of her office desk, then her hand opened feebly and lay palm upward and still" (*B* 80–81). Cousin Lymon skips town with Marvin Macy. Amelia waits for him for three years, and "in the fourth year ... Miss Amelia hired a Cheehaw carpenter and had him board up the premises, and there in those closed rooms she has remained ever since" (*B* 83). Amelia's potential for a true androgynous subjectivity is immured in the house, just as Biff turns away from his double vision to greet the morning. She becomes "unmanned": she lets her hair grow, her muscles shrink "until she was as thin as old maids.... Her voice was broken, soft, and sad as the wheezy whine of the church pump organ" (*B* 83), recalling the decline of Ovid's Hermaphroditus.[23]

That femininity has a castrating affect on the androgynous Miss Amelia and Biff Brannon underscores the observation that because "the woman's body stands for the signifier of lack, it follows that the [male] androgyne figure invariably evokes castration" (Pacteau 70). In the end, Biff comes closer to T.S. Eliot's Tiresias, an "old man with wrinkled dugs" (72),[24] because plenitude, as suggested by Biff's "Our Father," is problematically entangled with androgynous impotence. Thus, while Bakhtin's grotesque androgyny has birth arising from death, the fantasy of androgyny Biff Brannon enacts is, rather, "a narcissistic 'caress' in which the subject annihilates itself" (Pacteau 82), recalling the scene in *The Heart Is a Lonely Hunter* I discussed in the previous chapter where Biff stands before the mirror, gazing on his feminine self. The self-sufficient narcissism of the androgyne cannot be generative; beneath the omnipotence of the pregnant body is the threat of sterility, impotence. This is the descent into feminine castration that is the fate of the feminized man.

Another way in which *The Heart Is a Lonely Hunter* troubles the configuration of androgyny set out in *Rabelais and His World* and linked to the sterility of femininity is in its use of the tropes of ascent and descent. In his account of grotesque androgyny, Bakhtin insists on the centrality as well as the necessity of the role of the "material bodily lower stratum" (370), the location of genitals, bowels, womb, uterus, and thus creation: "To degrade ... means to concern oneself with the lower stratum of the body, the life of the belly and the reproductive organs; it therefore relates to acts of defecation and copulation, conception, pregnancy, and birth" (21). Ginsburg finds this movement problematic in that, like Ovid's Tiresias, "[t]he grotesque carnival body is degraded into the 'lower bodily stratum' associated with the feminine, and, in the same breath, is elevated into a principle of universal significance as the Material Body, no longer that of woman" (167). On the other hand, Bakhtin's image of feminine degradation to produce carnivalesque subjectivity could instead pose "a challenge to male transcendence through the generative power of female immanence" (Cullingford 21). However, in *The Heart Is a Lonely Hunter*, the movement of the male toward femininity is *upward*, not downward. That is to say, Biff Brannon *transcends* the bodily functions. As already noted, Biff "was scrupulously clean from the belt upwards. Every morning he soaped his chest and arms and neck and feet—and about twice during the season he got into the bathtub and cleaned all of his parts" (32). Biff is repulsed by or fearful of "the material bodily lower stratum"; it is not the fruitful resource Bakhtin claims is the pivot of the grotesque body.

Finally, *The Ballad of the Sad Café* directly takes issue with, to undermine, the equation grotesque–maternal–female. Miss Amelia Evans is unable to be contained within these terms and so unsettles any literal alignment of female body with maternal body. Amelia is a grotesque, not merely because she is a woman but because she is both like a man and unreproductive. In other words, her grotesqueness does not emanate from an unruly female pregnant body. One reader goes so far as to assert that Amelia is a literal *phallic* figure: that she is "ugly, oversized.... Elongated and masculine, suggests of course the phallus."[25] Although, as I have said, Amelia's rejection of her procreative duties is usually considered a major shortcoming, Russo astutely notes that "the distinction ... between the mother's body and the female body is absolutely crucial to feminist cultural criticism and reproductive politics" (119). The distinction opens up alternative possibilities for female subjectivity outside culturally perceived and required roles for, and functions of, women. In a similar way, the prepubescent girls along with the numerous childless adult women throughout McCullers's texts offer other good examples of the jamming of the female–maternal–grotesque equation.[26] The burden of the equation is thus replaced with a possibility that women, too, can participate in an open-ended form of subjectivity and need not merely function as the ground to man's representation. McCullers has created a new grotesque: Amelia's androgyny means that she is in excess of any exclusive gendered subjectivity, yet in her "barrenness" she suggests a lack of what it takes to be a woman. She both exceeds and falls short.

McCullers's texts produce new forms of grotesque subjectivity that hinge on contradiction, a type of subjectivity the figure of androgyny cannot contain. Having said this, however, it is worth noting once more the vigor with which several feminist commentators on McCullers's work reject the label "grotesque" when it is attached to Amelia. However, there is potential in reading McCullers's texts in terms of Bakhtin's concept of the grotesque. For example, as we have seen, McCullers's portraits of Biff and Miss Amelia might counter feminist anxiety vis-à-vis the appropriation of the feminine implied by Bakhtin's grotesque. The worry is, first, that women are excluded from carnivalesque subjectivity yet simultaneously provide the ground for the new male, and second, that the grotesque becomes too easily equated with both the maternal and female. To try and avoid the possible risks of feminine appropriation some feminists find located in the grotesque, it is useful to explore Bakhtin's rhetorical device of hybridization. This notion of hybridity more satisfactorily describes the friction of the "two in one" in McCullers's texts than does the hazardous trope of pregnancy.

Hybridity emerges from Bakhtin's discussion of dialogism in his essay "Discourse in the Novel." Strictly speaking, hybridity, according to Caryl Emerson and Michael Holquist, involves "[t]he mixing, within a single concrete utterance, of two or more different linguistic consciousnesses, often widely separated in time and social space.... [T]heir double-voicedness is not meant to resolve" (*Dialogic Imagination* 429).[27] Elizabeth Cullingford draws out from this the idea that "hybridization or the mixing of messages corresponds ... with a 'deconstructed' feminism, which undoes the binary oppositions of 'masculine' and 'feminine' in order to unsettle patriarchal prescriptions for gender identity" (26). Accordingly, gender identity is constantly being reviewed and reformed; hybridity produces not unity but "incompleteness, becoming, ambiguity, indefinability, non-canonicalism" (Clark and Holquist 312). It is, in fine, strictly antithetical to androgynous synthesis. Although the double-voiced hybrid is primarily a rhetorical device, its characteristics connote those of the grotesque in *Rabelais and His World*: "The essence of the grotesque is precisely to present a contradictory and double-faced fullness of life" (62). McCullers has a similar concept of the grotesquery of existence, which she defines as "the juxtaposition of the tragic with the humorous, the immense with the trivial, the sacred with the bawdy, the whole soul of man with a materialistic detail" ("Russian Realists" 258).

In *Rabelais and His World*, the hybrid appears in Rabelais's image of the hermaphrodite: "a man's body with two heads facing one another, four arms, four feet, a pair of arses and a brace of sexual organs, male and female" (323). Although Bakhtin calls this an image of androgyny, it is not concerned with synthesis, like classical androgyny, but with juxtaposition. A brief exploration of hermaphroditism illuminates both Bakhtin's concept of a hybrid "two bodies in one" and McCullers's world of irresolvable paradoxes. The hermaphrodite embodies an unstable and dynamic movement between two supposedly exclusive poles, male and female, thus differing from the androgyne, which seeks to smooth over (gender) difference in the name of the One.

Garber, pondering Jungian androgyny, concludes that there are "two kinds of androgyny, the good kind which was spiritual, mythical, 'archetypal,' and productive of intrapsychic oneness, and the bad kind, which was physical, sexy, and disturbing" (*Vice Versa* 211).[28] For, while the androgynous figure is a fantasy (it *seems* both male and female), the hermaphrodite is both, and so is a reality. In other words, the hermaphrodite is the "real" representation of "the impossible referent," the androgyne. Consequently, the hermaphrodite, with its "brace of sexual organs," is a freak, a grotesque; not a classical ideal, but an imperfect figure.

Kari Weil further clarifies the difference between static androgyny and truly grotesque hermaphroditism by drawing on Barthes's concepts of "paradoxism" and "antithesis."[29] She equates androgyny with antithesis, which is "a figure of stable opposition," a union of two halves. Hermaphroditism is closer to paradoxism, a hybrid figure of confusion that embodies "a more dynamic and unstable conflict." In the domain of gender, paradoxism, or hermaphroditism, is "created out of excess and the surpassing of boundaries" (35) and so "reveals both the instabilities of boundaries between categories of opposition such as masculine and feminine, and the self-serving function of their illusory symmetry" (12). Thus, like the hybrid, the hermaphrodite brings together, but not synthetically, elements usually kept ontologically separate. A true grotesque, the gender hybrid does not erase difference in the name of an androgynous synthesis. Instead, hybridity, like hermaphroditism, engages with—specifically sexual—difference, that is, it presents both genders at the same time, with the incessant jarring of a true paradoxism.

The figure of the hermaphrodite makes a brief appearance in *The Member of the Wedding*. Frankie and her cousin John Henry see "the Half-Man Half-Woman, a morphidite and a miracle of science" (27), on display in the Freak House. O'Connor also writes of the freak show hermaphrodite in "A Temple of the Holy Ghost." In both writers' texts, as I have already noted, the hermaphrodite becomes a symbol of the young girls' horror at the changing pubescent body.[30] However, perhaps even more powerfully, the hermaphrodite enacts a dynamic form of subjectivity. The freak of "A Temple of the Holy Ghost" tells its audience that "God made me this way.... I never done it to myself nor had a thing to do with it" (97). This might suggest, symbolically, that gendered identity is not an option but a constant pull between different subject positions. The point is that a tense, or disrupted, identity is a condition of being human in McCullers's work.

Although the real figure of the hermaphrodite does not feature outside of the freak show, and only then in one novel, its effects of unstable juxtaposition nevertheless do haunt McCullers's writings. The most obvious image might be John Henry's hermaphroditic vision of the perfect world where everyone would be "half boy and half girl" (*M* 116), or again, Biff Brannon's belief that "by nature all people are of both sexes" (*H* 119) . However, in the former, the image is the androgynous one whereby two complementary halves make up a whole; the latter evokes the fantasy, or psychic model, of androgyny as found, for instance, in Woolf's *A Room of One's Own*.

Rather, the notion of the "two in one," in which difference is maintained, occurs in McCullers's poem "Father, Upon Thy Image We Are Spanned": "Why are we split upon our double nature, how are we planned? / Father, upon what image are we spanned?.... Who said *it is finished* when Thy synthesis was just begun." McCullers imagines human being as split and, more pertinently, as unfinished; synthesis is impeded, so that androgyny is imperfect. The imperfect or ruptured unity allows for the viable tensions and shifts in identity set out in McCullers's texts.

The poem's notion of spanning, precluding any possibility of integration, further suggests the unfinished nature of human identity.

Spanning suggests not a blending but rather *a two at once*, evidenced further by the unfinished nature of God's human creation. In *Gyn/Ecology*, Mary Daly develops her own concept of spanning. A productive concept, spanning breaks "mind-numbing combinations" of which androgyny, the blending of two complementary halves, is her example. "Spanning splits," she continues, "involves something Other than attempting to fasten together two apparently opposite parts, on the mistaken assumption that these 'halves' will make a whole" (386, 387).[31] In a similar way, "Father, Upon Thy Image We Are Spanned" articulates not an androgynous synthesis but a state of incompletion in the spirit of a hybrid hermaphroditism.

There are moments in *The Heart Is a Lonely Hunter* and *The Ballad of the Sad Café* in which spanning occurs in the realm of gender, either on the body's surface as clothing or in behavior. This is not androgyny, in which masculinity and femininity wholly merge to ignore sexual differentiation in order to achieve a static "roundness of being." It is, rather, a carnivalesque process in which supposedly contradictory elements are juxtaposed in the one body, in the form of the double-voiced hybrid.

Accordingly, in McCullers's texts, the dynamic of "two bodies in one" reveals that masculine and feminine are neither mutually exclusive nor potentially synthetic. Masculinity and femininity are in a constant state of agitation in her work. In *The Member of the Wedding* this is epitomized in the visiting cards Frankie makes one evening with "*Miss F. Jasmine Addams, Esq.*, engraved with squinted letters" (61, emphasis added). There is no merging of the heterodox elements, masculine naming and feminine naming. Rather, there is an unsettled and unsettling "two" at odds. There is a similar conflict in Mick's attempts to perform "as a woman" toward the end of *The Heart Is a Lonely Hunter*. Unlike Frankie, Mick does not change her name to reflect her newly acquired "womanliness" and thus, like Frankie's visiting cards, confounds masculinity and femininity in terms of nomenclature. Another example of gender hybridity occurs in *The Member of the Wedding* when Berenice comments on Frankie's incongruous appearance in the gaudy orange satin dress she chooses to wear to her brother's wedding. The dress does not mix with her boy's haircut and her dirt-encrusted elbows (106–7). In this sense, the hybrid image once more conjures up the figure of the fool of carnival. As noted in the previous chapter, I deemed the tomboys "foolish" in their inability to carry out "proper" gender performance, that is, the appropriate mask slipped to reveal something else. In the previous examples of hybridity, the young girls are again analogous to the fool who misreads the norms of appropriate association, who mixes messages.

The hybrid as fool appears again in *The Heart Is a Lonely Hunter* when Biff Brannon puts the dead Alice's "perfume on his dark hairy armpits" (198).

Heterodox elements are brought disturbingly into play, but not in any complementary or symmetrical sense. Similarly, on the day of Miss Amelia's marriage to Marvin Macy, dressed in her mother's wedding gown, Amelia fumbles for the pocket of her overalls, in search of pipe and tobacco. Amelia also mixes messages when she wears her red dress on the Sabbath (*B* 31).

On another occasion, again in her red dress, Amelia warms herself by the stove: "She did not warm her backside modestly, lifting her skirt only an inch or two, as do most women when in public. There was not a grain of modesty about Miss Amelia.... Now as she stood warming herself, her red dress was pulled up quite high in the back so that a piece of her strong, hairy thigh could be seen" (*B* 71). The reader is forced to pause before this image of Amelia; she seems to be both man and woman. This is a perfect example of hybridity that defies the limits of the discretely gendered classical body to displace stable gender formation in terms of either/or. This occurs not in terms of an excluded half seeking wholeness, but more broadly in the juxtaposition of elements usually deemed mutually exclusive. Thus, what the hybrid moment neatly describes is the tension of grotesque subjectivity in McCullers's works and so points to the failure or impossibility of any stable identity.

The hybrid then, by its nature, is a figure of unsustainable disease. Proof of this uneasiness lies in the fact that in the case of the young tomboys, southern society will not tolerate their waywardness and instead requires that they submit to cultural demands for "womanliness." Biff Brannon returns to the daylight world of sober reason, "a sensible man." Amelia is confined to the boarded-up café. Similarly, some critics have sought to contain the energy of the hybrid "two in one" in the static figure of androgyny because it is a more manageable synthesis of masculine and feminine.[32] So, for example, because Amelia cannot easily be positioned within the taxonomic bounds of classical androgyny, she is usually dismissed as a freak in her disavowal of her womanly functions.

The grotesque image of the hybrid best illuminates the dynamics of juxtaposition that underpin all of McCullers's writings. McCullers herself writes that "[p]aradox is a clue to communication, for what is *not* often leads to the awareness of what *is*" ("Flowering Dream" 284).[33] Even if instances of hybridity are only momentary, they nevertheless fruitfully account for the unfinished beings in McCullers's novels. More than this, the hybrid opens up the possibility of new lines of flight, not in terms of escape or transcendence of the human, which classical androgyny promises, but in terms of the transformation of how the human is understood. This is the principle that has informed my rereading of McCullers throughout, arguing that a rich conceptualization of the grotesque lies at the heart of McCullers's exploration of the strangeness of being alive.

NOTES

1. The other two were two parts male and two parts female.

2. Freud refers to Plato's myth as a "theory" ("Beyond the Pleasure Principle" 331–32).

3. For various readings of Woolf's concept of androgyny, see Showalter, "Virginia Woolf and the Flight into Androgyny" (Showalter, *A Literature of Their Own* 263–97); Moi, "Introduction: Who's Afraid of Virginia Woolf? Feminist Readings of Woolf" (Moi 1–18); Weil 145–59. See also Woolf's essay "Coleridge as Critic" (Woolf, *Essays* 221–25).

4. For an account of this criticism, see Showalter, *A Literature of Their Own*; Secor.

5. Schor's term referring to the erasure of sexual difference so that "a single universal history is presumed to cover both sexes" ("Dreaming Dissymmetry" 107).

6. See also *H* 23–24, 119–20, 207.

7. The exceptions are White, who applies the term "androgynous" to Amelia as well as Biff (100); and Rechnitz, who describes her as "a mixture of man-woman" (459).

8. See Westling 123; Millichap, "Carson McCullers" 334.

9. See Box 122–23; Kestler 31; and Evans, *Carson McCullers* 47–48.

10. Biff's attraction to the adolescent Mick, who is "as much like an overgrown boy than a girl," is echoed in his daydreams of "thin naked little boys, the half-grown children" (*H* 119, 110).

11. Carr even suggests that he is the "true" (androgynous) Christ-figure of the novel (*Understanding Carson McCullers* 32). (Singer is more commonly regarded as the Christ-figure. See Evans, *Carson McCullers* 41; Durham; Schorer 278; M. Whitt 25.) For Christ as an androgynous figure, see Weil 64; Heilbrun, *Toward a Recognition* 17–20; Daly 88.

12. Dodd makes a similar claim: Biff's "sexual needs are answered by his supplying in himself the female as well as the male role" (208). Eisinger writes that after Alice's death, Biff "becomes the unitary expression of both the male and female principles" (249).

13. See also Taetzsch, who maintains that "his developing androgyny is still contaminated by Alice's presence" (193). Interestingly, in Ovid's account of Hermaphroditus, the feminine, in the form of Salmacis, is likewise considered a contaminant, but to manhood, not to a "developing androgyny" (93).

14. Even when Alice was alive, "there was no distinctive point about her on which he could fasten his attention.... When he was away from her there was no one feature that stood out in his mind and he remembered her as a complete, unbroken figure" (*H* 17–18).

15. This idea is also reflected in "Mortgaged Heart."

16. Hugh McPherson, "Carson McCullers: Lonely Huntress," *Tamarack Review* 11 (spring 1959) 31, quoted in Box 121; Eisinger 249.

17. On this point, see Carlton 60.

18. See also Bakhtin, *Rabelais* 21, 308. The notion of pregnancy is also apparent in Woolf's conceptualization of androgyny where she writes that "[i]t is when fusion takes place that the mind is fully fertilized" (*Room of One's Own* 92).

19. See also Bakhtin, *Rabelais* 25, 26, 50, 52, 92.

20. Note also that the mothers of Frankie and Miss Amelia died in childbirth.

21. See also Bakhtin, *Rabelais* 242, 243.

22. See also Russo 56, 63.

23. Amelia's case is interesting, for when she performs womanliness with a vengeance, she is at the height of her powers, as explored in the previous chapter. But when she becomes unmanned/castrated, she is left "only" a woman.

24. Dugs are human breasts that are withered and old, doubly emphasizing the unproductive, unnourishing figure of Tiresias. This image might also recall the old hags of *Rabelais*. However, it must be remembered that they are "pregnant."

25. Robert S. Phillips, "Painful Love: Carson McCullers's Parable," *Southwest Review* 51 (1966): 82, quoted in James 82.

26. For example, Alison Langdon and Leonora Penderton in *Reflections in a Golden Eye*, Alice Brannon in *The Heart Is a Lonely Hunter*, and Berenice Sadie Brown in *The Member of the Wedding*.

27. Stallybrass and White employ hybridity for their analysis of English cultural history and define it as the carnivalesque process of "inmixing" whereby "self and other become enmeshed in an inclusive, heterogeneous, dangerously unstable zone" (193).

28. See also Garber, *Vice Versa* 214, 218.

29. Weil also draws on Schlegel's distinction between two types of irony (31–59). Haraway's concept of irony is also useful here: "Irony is about contradictions that do not resolve into larger wholes, even dialectically, about the tension of holding incompatible things together because both or all are necessary and true" (65). See also Weil regarding Haraway and irony (160–61).

30. Like the freak show hermaphrodite in O'Connor's "A Temple of the Holy Ghost," McCullers's hermaphrodite remains clothed. See chapter 1 above for an account of the hermaphrodite as an adolescent fantasy. See Kahane, "Maternal Legacy," for an account of the hermaphrodite in O'Connor. See Westling for a comparison of the use to which O'Connor and McCullers put this figure.

31. Daly likens androgyny to an image of "John Travolta and Farrah Fawcett-Majors scotch-taped together" (xi).

32. An intriguing example is Rich, who takes great pains to assert Biff's masculinity in order to avoid any possibility that he might be a "deviant." She bends over backward to "justify" Biff's feminine operations: he sews because he is a "practical man and not confined by the chauvinistic attitude that it is woman's work"; his opulent decor reveals "aesthetic appreciation and a romantic nature"; he wears Alice's perfume as a reminder of the past. In sum, all Biff's feminine traits "reveal his strength; Jake [Blount] recognizes and respects this, for although he jeers at Biff about his being a capitalist, he never ridicules his perfume" (118–19).

33. Similarly, Flannery O'Connor believes that to "know oneself is, above all, to know what one lacks" (*Mystery and Manners* 35).

Chronology

1917	Lula Carson Smith is born on February 19 in Columbus, Georgia, to Lamar Smith and Marguerite Waters Smith.
1919	Brother Lamar Smith Jr. is born on May 13.
1922	Sister Margarita Gachet Smith is born August 2.
1930	Drops the use of "Lula" in her name.
1932	As a senior in high school, she suffers from rheumatic fever, which is thought to have contributed to her crippling strokes later in life.
1933	Graduates from Columbus High School. Writes plays and her first short story, "Sucker."
1934	Travels to New York City, where she enrolls in creative writing courses at Columbia University.
1935	Meets Reeves McCullers through mutual friend. Studies writing at New York University.
1936	First published story, "Wunderkind," appears in *Story* magazine. Becomes seriously ill, lives at home through the winter; starts work on "The Mute," which becomes *The Heart Is a Lonely Hunter*.
1937	On September 20 she marries Reeves McCullers. Moves into Reeves' apartment in Charlotte, North Carolina, and continues work on her novel.
1940	*The Heart Is a Lonely Hunter* is published. *Reflections in a*

Golden Eye is published in two parts in October and November in *Harper's Bazaar*. McCullers is ill during most of the winter.

1941   *Reflections in a Golden Eye* is published in book form. In February, McCullers is stricken with her first cerebral stroke. She initiates divorce proceedings against Reeves. First published poem, "The Twisted Trinity," appears in *Decision*. She suffers second major illness of the year with pleurisy, strep throat, and double pneumonia.

1942   Notified of award of Guggenheim Fellowship. "A Tree, a Rock, a Cloud" published in *Harper's* and selected for the annual *O. Henry Memorial Prize Stories* anthology.

1943   *The Ballad of the Sad Café* published in *Harper's Bazaar*. Awarded $1000 from the American Academy of Arts and Letters and the National Institute of Arts and Letters.

1944   McCullers suffers a severe nervous breakdown. Her father dies in August of a heart attack. She moves with her mother and Rita to Nyack, New York.

1945   On March 19, she remarries Reeves.

1946   Reeves is granted physical disability discharge from the army. *The Member of the Wedding* is published. She is awarded second Guggenheim Fellowship. Visits Tennessee Williams on Nantucket Island and begins rewriting *The Member of the Wedding* as a play. In autumn, she leaves for Europe with her husband; plan to live in Paris.

1947   McCullers suffers two serious strokes and is paralyzed on left side. In December, she is flown home because of paralysis, along with her husband who suffers from delirium.

1948   In March, she attempts suicide and is hospitalized in Manhattan.

1950   *The Member of the Wedding* opens on Broadway. It wins the New York Drama Critics' Circle Award for best play of the season as well as other awards.

1951   Sells screen rights to *The Member of the Wedding*. Her collected works are published as *The Ballad of the Sad Café and Other Works*.

1952   *The Ballad of the Sad Café and Collected Short Stories* are published. McCullers is inducted into the National

	Institute of Arts and Letters. She and Reeves purchase a home outside of Paris, France.
1953	Carson and Reeves experience marital problems. Reeves tries to convince her to commit a double suicide. In November, Reeves kills himself in a Paris hotel.
1955	Travels with Tennessee Williams to Key West in April to work on dramatizing three manuscripts. On June 10, McCullers's mother dies unexpectedly and she is utterly devastated.
1957	*The Square Root of Wonderful* opens on Broadway but closes after only forty-five performances.
1958	McCullers suffers acute depression over play's premature closing.
1959–62	Undergoes operations on arm, hand, and wrist as well as surgery for breast cancer. In 1961 *Clock Without Hands* is published. By 1962, she must spend most of her time in a wheelchair.
1963	"Sucker" is published. Edward Albee's adaptation of *The Ballad of the Sad Café* opens on Broadway.
1964	In the spring, she breaks her right hip and shatters left elbow. Collection of children's verses, *Sweet as a Pickle, Clean as a Pig* is published.
1966	Works on autobiography.
1967	On August 15, she suffers final stroke and is comatose for forty-seven days. Carson McCullers dies on September 29.
1968	Film version of *The Heart Is a Lonely Hunter* is released.
1971	Margarita G. Smith, Carson's sister, edits *The Mortgaged Heart*, a collection of Carson's short stories, poems, and essays.
1999	Unfinished autobiography, *Illumination and Night Glare*, edited by Carlos L. Dews, is published.

Contributors

HAROLD BLOOM is Sterling Professor of the Humanities at Yale University. He is the author of over 20 books, including *Shelley's Mythmaking* (1959), *The Visionary Company* (1961), *Blake's Apocalypse* (1963), *Yeats* (1970), *A Map of Misreading* (1975), *Kabbalah and Criticism* (1975), *Agon: Toward a Theory of Revisionism* (1982), *The American Religion* (1992), *The Western Canon* (1994), and *Omens of Millennium: The Gnosis of Angels, Dreams, and Resurrection* (1996). *The Anxiety of Influence* (1973) sets forth Professor Bloom's provocative theory of the literary relationships between the great writers and their predecessors. His most recent books include *Shakespeare: The Invention of the Human* (1998), a 1998 National Book Award finalist, *How to Read and Why* (2000), *Genius: A Mosaic of One Hundred Exemplary Creative Minds* (2002), and *Hamlet: Poem Unlimited* (2003). In 1999, Professor Bloom received the prestigious American Academy of Arts and Letters Gold Medal for Criticism, and in 2002 he received the Catalonia International Prize.

JOHN McNALLY teaches English at Wake Forest University. He is the editor of a few collections of short stories and also has written novels.

JOSEPH R. MILLICHAP teaches English at Western Kentucky University. He has published a book on Robert Penn Warren and another on the Southern Renaissance. He also has written poems and short stories

PANTHEA REID BROUGHTON has taught in the English Department at Virginia Polytechnic Institute and State University. She has published a book on William Faulkner, edited a book on Walker Percy, and co-authored *Literature: Fiction, Poetry, Drama*.

MARGARET B. McDOWELL has been Professor of Rhetoric at the University of Iowa, where she also taught in the women's studies program. She is the author of *Edith Wharton* and *Poems from the Heart*.

LOUISE WESTLING is in the English Department at the University of Oregon. She is the author of *Eudora Welty* and a book on Welty, McCullers, and Flannery O'Connor. She has published many essays on women writers and Southern literature.

MARY ANN DAZEY taught at Mississippi State University and has published on McCullers as well as Conrad.

RUTH M. VANDE KIEFT is a retired professor of English at Queens College, City University of New York. She is the author of *Eudora Welty* and the editor of *Thirteen Stories by Eudora Welty*; most of her critical writing has covered Southern writers.

MARGARET WHITT is Associate Professor in the English Department at the University of Denver, where she also is Director, Freshman English. She has published a book on Flannery O'Connor and another on Gloria Naylor.

CLARE WHATLING has taught at Manchester University and has published *Screen Dreams: Fantasizing Lesbians in Film*.

DOREEN FOWLER teaches at the University of Kansas. She is the author of a book on William Faulkner and has jointly edited several other titles on Faulkner as well.

SARAH GLEESON-WHITE is an independent scholar living in Sydney, Australia. She attended the University of New South Wales and is the author of *Strange Bodies: Gender and Identity in the Novels of Carson McCullers*.

Bibliography

Als, Hilton. "Unhappy Endings: The Collected Carson McCullers." *New Yorker* 77, no. 38 (December 3, 2001): 94–101.

Auchincloss, Louis. *Pioneers and Caretakers: A Study of Nine American Women Novelists*. Minneapolis: University of Minneapolis Press, 1965.

———. "Themes of Eros and Agape in the Major Fiction of Carson McCullers." *Pembroke Magazine* 20 (1988): 72–76.

Bigsby, C.W.E. "Edward Albee's Georgia Ballad." *Twentieth Century Literature* 13, no. 4 (January 1968): 229–36.

Bixby, George. "Carson McCullers: A Bibliographical Checklist."*American Book Collector* 5, no. 1 (January–February 1984): 38–43.

Box, Patricia S. "Androgyny and the Musical Vision: A Study of Two Novels by Carson McCullers." *Southern Quarterly* 16 (1978): 117–23.

Buchen, Irving. "Divine Collusion: The Art of Carson McCullers." *The Dalhousie Review* 54 (1974): 529–41.

Carlton, Ann. "Beyond Gothic and Grotesque: A Feminist View of Three Female Characters of Carson McCullers." *Pembroke Magazine* 20 (1988): 54–62.

Carr, Virginia Spencer. *Understanding Carson McCullers*. Columbia: University of South Carolina Press, 1990.

Carr, Virginia Spencer, and Joseph R. Millichap. "Carson McCullers." In *American Women Writers: Bibliographical Essays*, edited by Maurice Duke, Jackson Bryer, and M. Thomas Inge, 297–319. Westport, CT: Greenwood, 1983.

Chamlee, Kenneth. "Cafés and Community in Three Carson McCullers Novels." *Studies in Amerian Fiction.* 18 (1990): 233–240.

Clark, Beverly Lyon, and Melvin Friedman, eds. *Critical Essays on Carson McCullers.* London; New York: Prentice-Hall International, 1996.

Clark, Charlene Kerne. "Male-Female Pairs in Carson McCullers' *The Ballad of the Sad Café* and *The Member of the Wedding.*" *Notes on Contemporary Literature* 9, no. 1 (1979): 11–12.

Cook, Richard M. *Carson McCullers.* New York: Ungar, 1975.

Crocker, Halie. "Carson McCullers since 1980: A Bibliography." *Bulletin of Bibliography* 57, no. 3 (September 2000): pp. 153–57.

Dodd, Wayne D. "The Development of Theme Through Symbol in the Novels of Carson McCullers." *Georgia Review* 17, no.1 (Spring 1963): 206–13.

Doty, Kathleen. "Dialogue, Deixis, and Narration in a Dramatic Adaptation." *Poetica* 31 (1989): 42–59.

Edmonds, Dale. *Carson McCullers.* Austin: Steck-Vaughn, 1969.

Evans, Oliver. *Carson McCullers, Her Life and Work.* London: Owen, 1965.

———. "The Case of Carson McCullers." *Georgia Review* 18 (1964): 40–45.

Folk, Barbara Nauer. "The Sad Sweet Music of Carson McCullers." *Georgia Review* 16 (Summer 1962): 202–209.

Frazier, Adelaide. "Terminal Metaphors for Love." *Pembroke Magazine* 20 (1988): 77–81.

Gaillard, Dawson F. "The Presence of the Narrator in Carson McCullers' *The Ballad of the Sad Café.*" *Mississippi Quarterly* 25 (1972): 419–27.

Gaver, Lawrence. *Carson McCullers.* Minneapolis: University of Minneapolis Press, 1969.

Gervin, Mary A. "McCullers' Frames of Reference in 'The Ballad of the Sad Café.'" *Pembroke Magazine* 20 (1988): pp. 37–42.

Gossett, Louise Y. "Dispossessed Love: Carson McCullers." In *Violence in Recent Southern Fiction,* 159–77. Durham, N.C.: Duke University Press, 1965.

Griffith, Albert J. "Carson McCullers' Myth of the Sad Café." *Georgia Review* 21 (1967): 46–56.

Hamilton, Alice. "Loneliness and Alienation: The Life and Work of Carson McCullers." *Dalhousie Review* 50 (1970): 215–29.

Hannon, Charles. "*The Ballad of the Sad Café* and Other Stories of Women's Wartime Labor." In *Bodies of Writing, Bodies in Performance,* edited by Thomas Foster. New York: New York University Press, 1996.

Hendrick, George. "'Almost Everyone Wants to Be the Lover': The Fiction of Carson McCullers." *Books Abroad* 42 (1968): 389–391.

James, Judith Giblin. *Wunderkind: The Reputation of Carson McCullers, 1940–1990*. Columbia, SC: Camden House, 1995.

Johnstoneaux, Rephael B. "The Malformations of Love: 'The Ballad of the Sad Café.'" *Encyclia* 65 (1988): 103–11.

Knowles, A.S. Jr. "Six Bronze Petals and Two Red: Carson McCullers in the Forties." In *The Forties: Fiction, Poetry, Drama*, edited by Warren French. Deland, FL: Everett, 1969.

Matsudaira, Toko. "Some Transformations in 'The Ballad of the Sad Café.'" *Shoin Literary Review* 20 (1986): pp. 51–66.

McCullers, Carson. "The Flowering Dream: Notes on Writing." In *The Mortgaged Heart*, edited by Margarita G. Smith. Boston: Houghton-Mifflin, 1971.

McDowell, Margaret. *Carson McCullers*. New York: Twayne, 1980.

Moore, Janice T. "McCullers' *The Ballad of the Sad Café*." *Explicator* 29 (1970), Item 27.

Mukherjee, Srimati. "The Impoverishment of the Female Hero in 'The Ballad of the Sad Café.'" *Proceedings of the Philological Association of Louisiana* (1992): 105–109.

Nagpal, Pratibha. "The Element of Grotesque in *Reflections in a Golden Eye* and *The Ballad of the Sad Café* by Carson McCullers." *Panjab University Research Bulletin* 18, no. 2 (October 1987): 61–66.

Perry, Constance M. "Carson McCullers and the Female Wunderkind." *Southern Literary Journal* 19 (1986).

Phillips, Robert S. "Dinesen's 'Monkey' and McCullers' 'Ballad': A Study in Literary Affinity." *Studies in Short Fiction* 1 (1964): 184–190.

———. "Painful Love: Carson McCullers' Parable." *Southwest Review* 51 (1966): 80–86.

Portada, Arleen. "Sex-role Rebellion and the Failure of Marriage in the Fiction of Carson McCullers." *Pembroke Magazine* 20 (1988): 63–71.

Poston, David. "The Myth of the Explosion: Inverted Archetypes in the Fiction of Carson McCullers." *Mount Olive Review* 7 (Winter-Spring 1993–1994): 13–22.

Presley, Delma E. "Carson McCullers and the South." *Georgia Review* 28 (1974): 19–32.

Rechnitz, Robert M. "The Failure of Love: The Grotesque in Two Novels by Carson McCullers." *Georgia Review* (Winter 1968): 454–63.

Slabey, Robert M. "Carson McCullers' Allegory of Love." *Xavier Review* 13, no. 2 (Fall 1993): 47–59.

Sosnoski, Karen. "Society's Freaks: The Effects of Sexual Stereotyping in Carson McCullers' Fiction." *Pembroke Magazine* 20 (1988): 82–88.

Stanley, William T. "Carson McCullers: 1965–1969, a Selected Checklist." *Bulletin of Bibliography* 27 (1970): 91–93.

Walsh, Margaret. "Carson McCullers' Anti-Fairy Tale: 'The Ballad of the Sad Café.'" *Pembroke Magazine* 20 (1988): 43–48.

Westling, Louise. "Carson McCullers's Tomboys." *Southern Humanities Review*. 14 (1982): 339–50.

———. *Sacred Groves and Ravaged Gardens: The Fiction of Eudora Welty, Carson McCullers, and Flannery O'Connor.* Athens: University of Georgia Press, 1985.

Whittle, Amberys R. "McCullers' 'The Twelve Mortal Men' and 'The Ballad of the Sad Café.'" *American Notes and Queries* 18 (1980): 158–59.

Wu, Cynthia. "Expanding Southern Whiteness: Reconceptualizing Ethnic Difference in the Short Fiction of Carson McCullers." *Southern Literary Journal* 34, no. 1 (Fall 2001): 44–55.

Acknowledgments

"The Introspective Narrator in 'The Ballad of the Sad Café'" by John McNally. From *South Atlantic Bulletin* 38, no. 4 (November 1973): 40–44. © 1973 by the South Atlantic Modern Language Association. Reprinted by permission.

"Carson McCullers' Literary Ballad" by Joseph R. Millichap. From *The Georgia Review* 27, no. 3 (Fall 1973): 329–339. © 1973 by the University of Georgia. Reprinted by permission.

"Rejection of the Feminine in Carson McCullers' *The Ballad of the Sad Café*" by Panthea Reid Broughton. From *Twentieth Century Literature* 20, no. 1 (January 1974): 34–43. © 1974 by Hofstra University Press. Reprinted by permission.

"*The Ballad of the Sad Café (1943)*" by Margaret B. McDowell. From *Carson McCullers*: 65–79. © 1980 by G.K. Hall & Co. Reprinted by permission.

"Carson McCullers' Amazon Nightmare" by Louise Westling. From *Modern Fiction Studies* 28, no 3 (Autumn 1982): pp. 465–474. © 1982 by the Purdue Research Foundation. Reprinted by permission.

"Two Voices of the Single Narrator in *The Ballad of the Sad Café*" by Mary Ann Dazey. From *The Southern Literary Journal* 17, no. 2 (Spring

1985): pp. 33–40. © 1985 by the Department of English of the University of North Carolina at Chapel Hill. Reprinted by permission.

"The Love Ethos of Porter, Welty, and McCullers" by Ruth M. Vande Kieft. From *The Female Tradition in Southern Literature*, edited by Carol S. Manning: pp. 235–258. © 1993 by the Board of Trustees of the University of Illinois. Reprinted by permission.

"From Eros to Agape: Reconsidering the Chain Gang's Song in McCullers's 'Ballad of the Sad Café'" by Margaret Whitt. From *Studies in Short Fiction* 33, no. 1 (Winter 1996): pp. 119–122. © 1996 by Newberry College. Reprinted by permission.

"Reading Miss Amelia: critical strategies in the construction of sex, gender, sexuality, the gothic and the grotesque" by Clare Whatling. From *Modernist Sexualities*, edited by Hugh Stevens and Caroline Howlett: pp. 239–250. © 2000 by Manchester University Press. Reprinted by permission.

"Carson McCullers's Primal Scenes: *The Ballad of the Sad Café*" by Doreen Fowler. From *Critique* 43, no. 3 (Spring 2002): p. 260–270. © 2002 by the Helen Dwight Reid Educational Foundation. Reprinted by permission.

"Two Bodies in One: *The Heart Is a Lonely Hunter* and *The Ballad of the Sad Café*" by Sarah Gleeson-White. From *Strange Bodies: Gender and Identity in the Novels of Carson McCullers*: pp. 96–118. © 2003 by the University of Alabama Press. Reprinted by permission.

Index

Characters in literary works are indexed by first name followed by the title of the work in parentheses. Titles are often shortened, e.g., *Ballad* for *The Ballad of the Sad Café*.